Tales of My Landlord
by Walter Scott

Address:
HardPress
8345 NW 66TH ST #2561
MIAMI FL 33166-2626
USA
Email: info@hardpress.net

TALES OF MY LANDLORD.

VOL. II.   A

Ahora bien, dixo el Cura, traedme, senor huésped, aquesos libros, que los quiero ver.   Que me place, respondió el, y entrando, en su aposento, sacó dél una maletilla vieja cerrada con una cadenilla, y abriéndola, halló en ella tres libros grandes y unos papeles de muy buena letra escritos de mano.—DON QUIXOTE, Part I. Capitulo 32.

It is mighty well, said the priest; pray, landlord, bring me those books, for I have a mind to see them.   With all my heart, answered the host, and, going to his chamber, he brought out a little old cloke-bag, with a padlock and chain to it, and opening it, he took out three large volumes, and some manuscript papers written in a fine character.—JARVIS's *Translation.*

TALES OF MY LANDLORD,

COLLECTED AND ARRANGED

BY

JEDEDIAH CLEISHBOTHAM,

SCHOOLMASTER AND PARISH-CLERK OF GANDERCLEUGH.

Hear, Land o' Cakes and brither Scots,
Frae Maidenkirk to Jonny Groats',
If there's a hole in a' your coats,
  I rede ye tent it,
A chiel's amang you takin' notes,
  An' faith he'll prent it.
     BURNS.

IN THREE VOLUMES:—VOL. II.

PHILADELPHIA:

PRINTED AND PUBLISHED BY JAMES MAXWELL.

1820.

OLD MORTALITY.

OLD MORTALITY.

CHAPTER VI.

Yea, this man's brow, like to a tragic leaf,
Foretels the nature of a tragic volume. *Shakspeare.*

BEING at length rid of the housekeeper's presence, Morton made a collection of what he had
reserved from the provisions set before him, and
prepared to carry them to his concealed guest.
He did not think it necessary to take a light, being perfectly acquainted with every turn of the
road; and it was lucky he did not do so, for he
had hardly stepped beyond the threshold ere a
heavy trampling of horses announced, that the
body of cavalry, whose kettle-drums they had before heard, were in the act of passing along the
high-road which winds round the foot of the bank
on which the house of Milnwood was placed. He
heard the commanding officer distinctly give the
word *halt.* A pause of silence followed, interrupted only by the occasional neighing or pawing
of an impatient charger.

'Whose house is this?' said a voice in a tone
of authority and command.

'Milnwood, if it like your honour,' was the reply.

'Is the owner well affected?' said the inquirer,

'He complies with the orders of government, and frequents an indulged minister,' was the response.

'Hum! ay! Indulged? a mere mask for treason, very impolitically allowed to those who are too great cowards to wear their principles barefaced. —Had we not better send up a party and search the house, in case some of the bloody villains concerned in this heathenish butchery may be concealed in it?'

Ere Morton could recover from the alarm into which this proposal had thrown him, a third speaker rejoined, ' I cannot think it at all necessary; Milnwood is an infirm, hypochondriac old man, who never meddles with politics, and loves his money-bags and bonds better than any thing else in the world. His nephew, I hear, was at the wappin-schaw to-day, and gained the popinjay, which does not look like a fanatic. I should think they are all gone to bed long since, and an alarm at this time of night might kill the poor old man.'

' Well,' rejoined the leader, ' if that be so, to search the house would be lost time, of which we have but little to throw away. Gentlemen of the Life Guards, forward—March.'

A few notes on the trumpet, mingled with the occasional boom of the kettle-drum, to mark the cadence, joined with the tramp of hoofs and the clash of arms, announced that the troop had resumed its march. The moon broke out as the leading files of the column attained a hill up which the road winded, and showed indistinctly the glittering of the steel-caps; and the dark figures of the horses and riders might be imperfectly traced through the gloom. They continued to advance up the hill, and sweep over the top of it in such long succession, as intimated a considerable numerical force.

When the last of them had disappeared, young Morton resumed his purpose of visiting his guest. Upon entering the place of refuge, he found him seated on his humble couch, with a pocket-bible open in his hand, which he seemed to study with intense meditation. His broadsword, which he had unsheathed in the first alarm at the arrival of the dragoons, lay naked across his knees, and the little taper that stood beside him upon the old chest, which served the purpose of a table, threw a partial and imperfect light upon those stern and harsh features, in which ferocity was rendered more solemn and dignified by a wild cast of tragic enthusiasm. His brow was that of one in whom some strong o'er-mastering principle has overwhelmed all other passions and feelings, like the swell of a high spring-tide, when the usual cliffs and breakers vanish from the eye, and their existence is only indicated by the chafing foam of the waves that burst and wheel over them. He raised his head, after Morton had contemplated him for about a minute.

‘ I perceive,’ said Morton, looking at his sword, ‘ that you heard the horsemen ride by; their passage delayed me for some minutes.’

‘ I scarcely heeded them,’ said Balfour; ‘ my hour is not yet come. That I shall one day fall into their hands, and be honourably associated with the saints whom they have slaughtered, I am full well aware. And I would, young man,

that the hour were come; it should be as welcome
to me as ever wedding to bridegroom.   But if
my Master has more work for me on earth, I
must not do his labour grudgingly.

'Eat and refresh yourself,' said Morton; 'to
morrow your safety requires you should leave
this place, in order to gain the hills, so soon as
you can see to distinguish the track through the
morasses.'

'Young man,' returned Balfour, 'you are already weary of me, and would be yet more so,
perchance, did you know the task upon which I
have been lately put.   And I wonder not that it
should be so, for there are times when I am weary of myself.   Think you not it is a sore trial for
flesh and blood, to be called upon to execute the
righteous judgments of Heaven while we are yet
in the body, and retain that blinded sense and
sympathy for carnal suffering which makes our
own flesh thrill when we strike a gash upon the
body of another?   And think you, that when
some prime tyrant has been removed from his
place, that the instruments of his punishment can
at all times look back on their share in his down-
fall with firm and unshaken nerves? Must they not
sometimes even question the truth of that inspiration which they have felt and acted under?
Must they not sometimes doubt the origin of that
strong impulse with which their prayers for heavenly direction under difficulties have been in-
wardly answered and confirmed, and confuse, in
their disturbed apprehensions, the responses of
Truth itself with some strong delusion of the enemy?'

' These are subjects, Mr. Balfour, on which I am ill qualified to converse with you,' answered Morton; ' but I own I should strongly doubt the origin of any inspiration which seemed to dictate a line of conduct contrary to those feelings of natural humanity, which Heaven has assigned to us as the general law of our conduct.'

Balfour seemed somewhat disturbed, and drew himself hastily up, but immediately composed himself, and answered coolly, ' It is natural you should think so; you are yet in the dungeon-house of the law, a pit darker than that into which Jeremiah was plunged, even the dungeon of Malcaiah the son of Hamelmelech, where there was no water but mire. Yet is the seal of the covenant upon your forehead, and the son of the righteous, who resisted to blood where the banner was spread on the mountains, shalt not be utterly lost as one of the children of darkness. Trow ye, that in this day of bitterness and calamity, nothing is required at our hands but to keep the moral law as far as our carnal frailty will permit? Think ye our conquests must be only over our corrupt and evil affections and passions? No; we are called upon, when we have girded up our loins, to run the race boldly, and when we have drawn the sword, we are enjoined to smite the ungodly, though he be our neighbour, and the man of power and cruelty, though he were of our own kindred and the friend of our bosom.'

' These are the sentiments,' said Morton, ' that your enemies impute to you, and which palliate, if they do not exculpate, the cruel measures which the council have directed against you. They af-

firm, that you pretend to inward light, rejecting
the restraints of legal magistracy, of national law,
and even of common humanity, when in opposition to what you call the spirit within you.'

'They do us wrong,' answered the Covenanter;
'it is they, perjured as they are, who have rejected all law, both divine and civil, and who now
persecute us for adherence to the solemn league
and covenant between God and the kingdom of
Scotland, to which all of them have sworn in
former days, save a few popish malignants, and
which they now burn in the market-places, and
tread under foot in derision. When this Charles
Stuart returned to these kingdoms, did the malignants bring him back? They had tried it with
strong hand, but they failed, I trow. Could
James Grahame of Montrose and his Highland
catterans have put him again in the place of his
father? I think their heads on the Wesport told
another tale for many a long day. It was the
workers of the glorious work—the reformers of
the beauty of the tabernacle, that called him again
to the high place from which his father fell. And
what has been our reward? In the words of the
prophet, " We looked for peace, but no good came;
and for a time of health, and behold trouble—
The snorting of his horses was heard from Dan;
the whole land trembled at the sound of the neighing of his strong ones; for they are come, and
have devoured the land and all that is in it." '

'Mr. Balfour,' answered Morton, 'I neither
undertake to subscribe to or refute your complaints against the government. I have endeavoured to repay a debt due to the comrade of my

father, by giving you shelter in your distress, but you will excuse my engaging myself either in your cause, or in controversy. 1 will leave you to repose, and heartily wish it were in my power to render your condition more comfortable.'

'But I shall see you, I trust, in the morning, ere I depart?—I am not a man whose bowels yearn after kindred and friends of this world. When I put my hand to the plough, I entered into a covenant with my worldly affections that I should not look back on the things I left behind me. Yet the son of mine ancient comrade is to me as mine own, and I cannot behold him without the deep and firm belief, that I shall one day see him gird on his sword in the dear and precious cause for which his father fought and bled.'

With a promise on Morton's part that he would call the refugee when it was time for him to pursue his journey, they parted for the night.

Morton retired to a few hours rest; but his imagination, disturbed by the events of the day, did not permit him to enjoy sound repose. There was a blended vision of horror before him, in which his new friend seemed to be a principal actor. The fair form of Edith Bellenden also mingled in his dream, weeping, and with dishevelled hair, and appearing to call on him for comfort and assistance which he had it not in his power to render. He awoke from these unrefreshing slumbers with a feverish impulse, and a heart which foreboded disaster. There was already a tinge of dazzling lustre on the verge of the distant hills, and the dawn was abroad in all the freshness of a summer morning.

' I have slept too long,' he exclaimed to himself, ' and must now hasten to forward the journey of this unfortunate fugitive.'

He dressed himself as fast as possible, opened the door of the house with as little noise as he could, and hastened to the place of refuge occupied by the Covenanter. Morton entered on tiptoe, for the determined tone and manner, as well as the unusual language and sentiments of this singular individual, had struck him with a sensation approaching to awe. Balfour was still asleep. A ray of light streamed on his uncurtained couch, and showed to Morton the working of his harsh features, which seemed agitated by some strong internal cause of disturbance. He had not undressed. Both his arms were above the bed-cover, the right hand strongly clenched, and occasionally making that abortive attempt to strike which usually attends dreams of violence; the left was extended, and agitated, from time to time, by a movement as if repulsing some one. The perspiration stood on his brow, ' like bubbles in a late disturbed stream,' and these marks of emotion were accompanied with broken words which escaped from him at intervals—' Thou art taken Judas—thou art taken—Cling not to my knees—cling not to my knees—hew him down! —A priest? Ay, a priest of Baal, to be bound and slain, even at the brook Kishon—Fire-arms will not prevail against him—Strike—thrust with the cold iron—put him out of pain—put him out of pain, were it but for the sake of his gray hairs.'

Much alarmed at the import of these expressions, which seemed to burst from him even in sleep with the stern energy accompanying the perpetration of some act of violence, Morton shook his guest by the shoulder in order to wake him. The first words he uttered were, ' Bear me where ye will, I will avouch the deed.'

His glance around having then fully awakened him, he at once assumed all the stern and gloomy composure of his ordinary manner, and throwing himself on his knees before speaking to Morton, poured forth an ejaculatory prayer for the suffering Church of Scotland, entreating that the blood of her murdered saints and martyrs might be precious in the sight of Heaven, and that the shield of the Almighty might be spread over the scattered remnant, who, for His name's sake, were abiders in the wilderness. Vengeance—speedy and ample vengeance on the oppressors, was the concluding petition of his devotions, which he expressed aloud in strong and emphatic language, rendered more impressive by the orientalism of Scripture.

When he had finished his prayer, he arose, and taking Morton by the arm, they descended together to the stable, where the Wanderer, (to give Burley a title which was often conferred on his sect,) began to make his horse ready to pursue his journey. When the animal was saddled and bridled, Burley requested Morton to walk with him a gun-shot into the wood, and put him upon the right road for gaining the moors. Morton readily complied, and they walked for some time in silence under the shade of some fine old trees, pursuing a sort of natural path, which, after passing through woodland for about half a mile, led

into the bare and wild country which extends to
the foot of the hills.

At length Burley suddenly asked Morton,
' Whether the words he had spoken over-night
had borne fruit in his mind?'

Morton answered, ' That he remained of the
same opinion which he had formerly held, and
was determined, at least as far and as long as possible, to unite the duties of a good Christian with
those of a peaceful subject.'

' In other words,' replied Burley, ' you are desirous to serve both God and Mammon—to be
one day professing the truth with your lips, and
the next day in arms, at the command of carnal
and tyrannic authority, to shed the blood of those
who for the truth have forsaken all things? Think
ye,' he continued, ' to touch pitch, and remain
undefiled? to mix in the ranks of malignants, papists; papa-prelatists, latitudinarians, and scoffers;
to partake of their sports, which are like the
meals offered unto idols; to hold intercourse, perchance, with their daughters, as the sons of God
with the daughters of men in the world before
the flood, and yet to remain free from pollution?
I say unto you that all communication with the
enemies of the Church is the accursed thing which
God hateth! Touch not—taste not—handle not!
And grieve not, young man, as if you alone were
called upon to subdue your carnal affections, and
renounce the pleasures which are a snare to your
feet—I say to you, that the son of David hath
denounced no better lot on the whole generation
of mankind.'

He then mounted his horse, and, turning to Morton, repeated the text of Scripture, ' An heavy yoke was ordained for the sons of Adam from the day they go out of their mother's womb till the day that they return to the mother of all things; from him who is clothed in blue silk and weareth a crown, even to him who weareth simple linen,—wrath, envy, trouble, and unquietness, rigour, strife, and fear of death in the time of rest.'

Having uttered these words he set his horse into motion, and soon disappeared among the boughs of the forest.

' Farewell, stern enthusiast,' said Morton, looking after him; ' in some moods of my mind, how dangerous would be the society of such a companion!' If I am unmoved by his zeal for abstract doctrines of faith, or rather for a peculiar mode of worship, (such was the purport of his reflections,) can I be a man, and a Scotchman, and look with indifference on that persecution which has made wise men mad? Was not the cause of freedom, civil and religious, that for which my father fought; and shall I do well to remain inactive, or to take the part of an oppressive government, if there should appear any rational prospect of redressing the insufferable wrongs to which my miserable countrymen are subjected?— And yet who shall warrant me that these people, rendered wild by persecution, would not, in the hour of victory, be as cruel and as intolerant as those by whom they are now hunted down? What degree of moderation, or of mercy, can be expected from this Burley, so distinguished as one of their principal champions, and who seems even now to be reeking from some recent deed of violence, and to feel stings of remorse, which even his enthusiasm cannot altogether stifle? I am weary of seeing nothing but violence and fury around me—now assuming the mask of lawful authority, now taking that of religious zeal. I am sick of my country—of myself—of my dependent situation—of my repressed feelings—of these woods—of that river—of that house—of all but Edith; and she can never be mine. Why should I haunt her walks?—Why encourage my own delusion and perhaps hers?—she can never be mine. Her mother's pride—the opposite principles of our families—my wretched state of dependence—a poor miserable slave, for I have not even the wages of a servant—all circumstances give the lie to the vain hope that we can ever be united. Why then protract a delusion so painful?

'But I am no slave,' he said aloud, and drawing himself up to his full stature—' no slave, in one respect, surely. I can change my abode—my father's sword is mine, and Europe lies open before me, as before him and hundreds besides of my countrymen who have filled it with the fame of their exploits. Perhaps some lucky chance may raise me to a rank with our Ruthvens, our Lesleys, our Monroes, the chosen leaders of the famous Protestant champion; or, if not, a soldier's life or a soldier's grave.'

When he had formed this determination, he found himself near the door of his uncle's house, and resolved to lose no time in making him acquainted with it.

' Another glance of Edith's eye, another walk by Edith's side, and my resolution would melt away. I will take an irrevocable step, and then see her for the last time.'

In this mood he entered the wainscotted parlour, in which his uncle was already placed at his morning's refreshment, a huge plate of oatmeal porridge, with a corresponding allowance of butter-milk. The favourite housekeeper was in attendance, half standing, half resting on the back of a chair, in a posture betwixt freedom and respect.

The old gentleman had been remarkably tall in his earlier days, an advantage which he now lost by stooping to such a degree, that at a meeting, where there was some dispute concerning the sort of arch which should be thrown over a considerable brook, a facetious neighbour proposed to offer Milnwood a handsome sum for his curved backbone, alleging that he would sell any thing that belonged to him. Splay feet of unusual size, long thin hands, garnished with nails which seldom felt the steel, a wrinkled and puckered visage, the length of which corresponded with that of his person, together with a pair of little sharp bargain-making gray eyes, that seemed eternally looking out for their advantage, completed the highly unpromising exterior of Mr. Morton of Milnwood. As it would have been very injudicious to have lodged a liberal or benevolent disposition in such an unworthy cabinet, nature had suited his person with a mind exactly in conformity with it, that is to say, mean, selfish, and covetous.

When this amiable personage was aware of the presence of his nephew, he hastened, before addressing him, to swallow the spoonful of porridge which he was in the act of conveying to his mouth, and, as it chanced to be scalding hot, the pain occasioned by its descent down his throat and into his stomach, inflamed the ill humour with which he was already prepared to meet his kinsman.

'The de'il take them that made them,' was his first ejaculation, apostrophizing his mess of porridge.

'The're gude parritch enough,' said Mrs. Wilson, 'if ye wad but take time to sup them. I made them mysel; but if folk winna hae patience, they should get their thrapples causewayed.'

'Haud your peace, Alison, I was speaking to my nevoy.—How is this, sir? And what sort o' scampering gates are these o' going on? Ye were not at hame last night till near midnight.'

'Thereabouts, sir, I believe,' answered Morton, in an indifferent tone.

'Thereabouts, sir?—What sort of an answer is that, sir? Why came ye na hame when other folk left the grund?'

'I suppose you know the reason very well, sir,' said Morton; 'I had the fortune to be the best marksman of the day, and remained, as is usual, to give some little entertainment to the other young men.'

'The deevil ye did, sir! And ye come to tell me that to my face? You pretend to gi'e entertainments, that canna come by a dinner except by sorning on a carefu' man like me? But if ye put me to charges, I'se work it out o' ye. I see na why ye shouldna haud the pleugh, now that the pleughman has left us; it wad set ye better than wearing thae green duds, and wasting your siller on powther and lead; it wad put ye in an honest calling, and wad keep ye in bread without being uphauden to ony ane.'

'I am very ambitious of learning such a calling, sir, but I don't understand driving the plough.'

'And what for no? It's easier than your gunning and archery that ye like sae weel. Auld Davie is ca'ing it e'en now, and ye may be goadsman for the first twa or three days, and tak tent ye dinna o'er-drive the owsen, and then ye will be fit to gang between the stilts. Ye'll ne'er learn younger, I'll be your caution—Haggie-holm is heavy land, and Davie is ower auld to keep the coulter down now.'

'I beg pardon for interrupting you, sir, but I have formed a scheme for myself, which will have the same effect of relieving you of the burden and charge attending my company.'

'Ay? Indeed? a scheme o' yours? that must be a denty ane!' said the uncle, with a very peculiar sneer; 'let's hear about it, lad.'

'It is said in two words, sir. I intend to leave this country, and serve abroad, as my father did before these unhappy troubles broke out at home. His name will not be so entirely forgotten in the countries where he served but that it will procure his son at least the opportunity of trying his fortune as a soldier.'

'Gude be gracious to us!' exclaimed the housekeeper, 'our young Mr. Harry gang abroad?—na, na! eh, na! that maun never be.'

Milnwood, entertaining no thought or purpose of parting with his nephew, who was, moreover, very useful to him in many respects, was thunderstruck at this abrupt declaration of independence from a person whose deference to him had hitherto been unlimited. He recovered himself, however, immediately.

'And wha do you think is to give you the means, young man, for such a wild-goose chase? Not I, I am sure. I can hardly support you at hame. And ye wad be marrying, I'se warrant, as your father did afore ye, too, and sending your uncle hame a pack o' weans to be fighting and skirling through the house in my auld days, and to take wing and flee aff like yoursel, whenever they were asked to serve a turn about the town.'

'I have no thoughts of ever marrying,' answered Henry.

'Hear till him now!' said the housekeeper. 'It's a shame to hear a douce young lad speak in that way, since a' the warld kens that they maun either marry or do waur.'

'Haud your peace, Alison,' said her master; 'and you, Harry, put this nonsense out o' your head——this comes o' letting ye gang a sodgering for a day——mind ye hae nae siller, lad, for ony sic nonsense plans.'

'I beg your pardon, sir, my wants shall be very few; and would you please to give me the gold chain which the Margrave gave to my father after the battle of Lutzen"——

'Mercy on us! the gowd chain?' exclaimed his uncle.

'The chain of gowd!' re-echoed the house-keeper, both aghast with astonishment at the audacity of the proposal.

'I will keep a few links to remind me of him by whom it was won, and the place where he won it,' continued Morton; 'the rest shall furnish me the means of following the same career in which my father obtained that mark of distinction.'

'Mercifu' powers!' said the governante, 'my master wears it every Sunday.'

'Sunday and Saturday,' added old Milnwood, 'whenever I put on my black velvet coat; and Wylie Mactrickit is partly of opinion it's a kind of heir-loom, that rather belangs to the head of the house than to the immediate descendant. It has three thousand links; I have counted them a thousand times. It's worth three hundred pounds sterling.'

'That is more than I want, sir; if you choose to give me the third part of the money, and five links of the chain, it will amply serve my purpose, and the rest will be some slight atonement for the expense and trouble I have put you to.'

'The laddie's in a creel!' exclaimed his uncle. 'O, sirs, what will become o' the rigs o' Miln-wood when I am dead and gane! He would fling the crown of Scotland awa, if he had it.'

'Hout, sir,' said the old housekeeper, 'I maun e'en say it's partly your ain faut. Ye mauna curb his head ower sair in neither; and, to be sure, since he *has* gane doun to the Howff, ye maun just e'en pay the lawing.'

'If it be not abune twa dollars, Alison,' said the old gentleman, very reluctantly.

'I'll settle it mysel wi' Niel Blane, the first time I gang down to the clachan,' said Alison, 'cheaper than your honour or Mr. Harry can do;' and then whispered to Harry, 'dinna vex him ony mair, I'll pay the lave out o' the butter siller, and nae mair words about it.' Then proceeding aloud, 'And ye mauna speak o' the young gentleman hauding the pleugh; there's puir distressed whigs enow about the country will be glad to do that for a bite and a soup—it sets them far better than the like o' him.'

'And then we'll hae the dragoons on us,' said Milnwood, 'for comforting and entertaining intercommuned rebels, a bonny strait ye wad put us in!—But take your breakfast, Harry, and then lay by your new green coat, and put on your Raploch gray; it's a mair mensefu' and thrifty dress, and a mair seemly sight, than thae dangling slops and ribbands.'

Morton left the room, perceiving plainly that he had at present no chance of gaining his purpose, and, perhaps, not altogether displeased at the obstacles which seemed to present themselves to his leaving the neighbourhood of Tillietudlem. The housekeeper followed him into the next room, patting him on the back, and bidding him be a gude bairn, and pit by his braw things.

'And I'll loop doun your hat, and lay by the band and ribband,' said the officious dame; 'and ye maun never, at no hand, speak o' leaving the land, or of selling the gowd chain, for your uncle has an unco pleasure in looking on you, and in counting the links of the chainzie; and ye ken auld folk canna last for ever; sae the chain, and the lands, and a' will be your ain ae day; and ye may marry ony leddy in the country-side ye like, and keep a braw house at Milnwood, for there's enow o' means; and is not that worth waiting for, my dow?'

There was something in the latter part of the prognostic which sounded so agreeably in the ears of Morton, that he shook the old dame cordially by the hand, and assured her he was much obliged by her good advice, and would weigh it carefully before he proceeded to act upon his former resolution.

CHAPTER VII.

From seventeen years till now, almost fourscore,
Here lived I, but now live here no more.
At seventeen years many their fortunes seek,
But at fourscore it is too late a week.   *As you like it.*

WE must conduct our readers to the Tower of Tillietudlem, to which Lady Margaret Bellenden had returned, in romantic phrase, malcontent and full of heaviness, at the unexpected, and, as she deemed it, indelible affront, which had been brought upon her dignity by the public miscarriage of Goose Gibbie. That unfortunate man-at-arms was forthwith commanded to drive his feathered charge to the most remote parts of the common moor, and on no account to awaken the grief or resentment of his lady, by appearing in her presence while the sense of the affront was yet recent.

The next proceeding of Lady Margaret was to hold a solemn court of justice, to which Harrison and the butler were admitted, partly on the footing of witnesses, partly as assessors, to inquire into the recusancy of Cuddie Headrigg the ploughman, and the comfort and abetment which he had received from his mother, these being regarded as the original causes of the disaster which had befallen the chivalry of Tillietudlem. The charge being fully made out and substantiated, Lady Margaret resolved to reprimand the culprits in person, and, if she found them impenitent, to extend the censure into a sentence of expulsion from the barony. Miss Bellenden alone ventured to say any thing in behalf of the accused, but her countenance did not profit them as it might have done on any other occasion. For so soon as Edith had heard it ascertained that the unfortunate cavalier had not suffered in his person, his disaster had affected her with an irresistible disposition to laugh, which, in spite of Lady Margaret's indignation, or rather irritated, as usual, by restraint, had broke out repeatedly on her return homeward, until her grandmother, in no shape imposed upon by the several fictitious causes which the young lady assigned for her ill-timed risibility, upbraided her in very bitter terms with being insensible to the honour of her family. Miss Bellenden's intercession, therefore, had, on this occasion, little chance to be listened to.

As if to evince the rigour of her disposition, Lady Margaret, upon this solemn occasion, exchanged the ivory-headed cane with which she commonly walked, for an immense gold-headed staff which had belonged to her father, the deceased Earl of Torwood, and which, like a sort of mace of office, she only made use of upon occasions of special solemnity. Supported by this awful baton of command, Lady Margaret Bellenden entered the cottage of the delinquents.

There was an air of consciousness about old Mause, as she rose from her wicker chair in the chimney-nook, not with the cordial alertness of visage which used, on other occasions, to express the honour she felt in the visit of her lady, but with a certain solemnity and embarrassment, like an accused party on his first appearance in presence of his judge, before whom he is, nevertheless, determined to assert his innocence. Her arms were folded, her mouth primmed into an expression of respect, mingled with obstinacy, her whole mind apparently bent up to the solemn interview. With her best curtesy to the ground, and a mute motion of reverence, Mause pointed to the chair, which, on former occasions, Lady Margaret (for the good lady was somewhat of a gossip) had deigned to occupy for half an hour sometimes at a time, hearing the news of the country and of the borough. But at present her mistress was far too indignant for such condescension. She rejected the mute invitation with a haughty wave of her hand, and drawing herself up as she spoke, she uttered the following interrogatory in a tone calculated to overwhelm the culprit.

'Is it true, Mause, as I am informed by Harrison, Gudyill, and others of my people, that you ha'e

ta'en it upon you, contrary to the faith you owe
to God and the king, and to me, your natural
lady and mistress, to keep back your son frae the
wappen-schaw, held by the order of the sheriff,
and to return his armour and abuilyiements at a
moment when it was impossible to find a suitable delegate in his stead, whereby the barony of
Tillietudlem, baith in the person of its mistress
and indwellers, has incurred sic a disgrace and
dishonour as hasna befa'en the family since the
days of Malcolm Canmore?'

Mause's habitual respect for her mistress was
extreme; she hesitated, and one or two short
coughs expressed the difficulty she had in defending herself.

' I am sure—my leddy—hem, hem!—I am sure
I am sorry—very sorry that ony cause of displeasure should hae occurred—but my son's illness'—

' Dinna tell me of your son's illness, Mause!
Had he been sincerely unweel, ye would ha'e
been at the Tower by daylight to get something
that wad do him gude; there are few ailments
that I have nae medical recipes for, and that ye
ken fu' weel.'

' O ay, my leddy! I am sure ye hae wrought
wonderfu' cures; the last thing ye sent Cuddie
when he had the batts, e'en wrought like a
charm.'

' Why, then, woman, did ye not apply to me, if
there was ony real need?—But there was none, ye
fause-hearted vassal that ye are!'

' Your leddyship never ca'd me sic a word as
that before. Ohon! that I suld live to be ca'd

sae,' she continued, bursting into tears, ' and me a born servant o' the house o' Tillietudlem! I am sure they belie baith Cuddie and me sair if they said he wad na' fight ower boots and blude for your leddyship and Miss Edith, and the auld Tower—ay suld he, and I would rather see him buried beneath it, than he suld gi'e way—but thir ridings and wappen-schawings, my leddy, I hae nae broo o' them ava. I can find nae warrant for them whatsoever.'

' Nae warrant for them? Do ye na ken, woman, that ye are bound to be liege vassals in all hunting, hosting, watching, and warding, when lawfully summoned thereto in my name? Your service is no gratuitous. I trow ye hae land for it.—Ye're kindly tenants; hae a cot-house, a kale-yard, and a cow's grass on the common.— Few hae been brought farther ben, and ye grudge your son suld gi'e me a day's service in the field?'

' Na, my leddy—na, my leddy, it's no that,' exclaimed Mause, greatly embarrassed, ' but ain canna serve twa maisters; and, if the truth maun e'en come out, there's Ane abune whase commands I maun obey before your leddyship's. I am sure I would put neither king's nor kaisar's, nor ony earthly creature's afore them.'

' How mean ye by that, ye auld fule woman?— D'ye think that I order ony thing against conscience?'

' I dinna pretend to say that, my leddy, in regard o' your leddyship's conscience, which has been brought up, as it were, wi' prelatic principles, but ilka ane maun walk by the light o' their ain; and mine,' said Mause, waxing bolder as the conference became animated, ' tells me that I suld leave a'—cot, kale-yard, and cow's grass,— and suffer a', rather than that I or mine should put on harness in an unlawfu' cause.'

' Unlawfu'!' exclaimed her mistress; ' the cause to which you are called by your lawfu' leddy and mistress—by the command of the king—by the writ of the privy council—by the order of the lord lieutenant—by the warrant of the sheriff!'

' Ay, my leddy, nae doubt; but, no to displeasure your leddyship, ye'll mind that there was ance a king in Scripture they ca'd Nebuchadnezzar, and he set up a golden image in the plain o' Dura, as it might be in the haugh yonder by the waterside, where the array were warned to meet yesterday; and the princes and the governors, and the captains, and the judges themsels, forbye the treasurers, the counsellors, and the sheriffs, were warned to the dedication thereof, and commanded to fall down and worship at the sound of the cornet, flute, harp, sackbut, psaltery, and all kinds of music.'

' And what o' a' this, ye fule wife? Or what had Nebuchadnezzer to do with the wappenschaw of the Upper Ward of Clydesdale?'

' Only just thus far, my leddy,' continued Mause, firmly, ' that prelacy is like the great golden image in the plain of Dura, and that as Shadrach, Meshach, and Abednego were borne out in refusing to bow down and worship, so neither shall Cuddy Headrigg, your leddyship's poor pleughman, at least wi' his auld mither's consent, make murgeons or jenny-flections, as they ca' them, in the house of the prelates and curates, nor gird him wi' armour to fight in their cause, either at the sound of kettle-drums, organs, bagpipes, or ony other kind of music whatever.'

Lady Margaret Bellenden heard this exposition of Scripture with the greatest possible indignation as well as surprise.

' I see which way the wind blaws,' she exclaimed, after a pause of astonishment; ' the evil spirit of the year sixteen hundred and forty-twa is at wark again as merrily as ever, and ilka auld wife in the chimley-neuck will be for knapping doctrine wi' doctors o' divinity and the godly. fathers o' the church.'

' If your leddyship means the bishops and curates, I'm sure they hae been but stepfathers to the kirk o' Scotland. And, since your leddyship is pleased to speak o' parting wi' us, I am free to tell you a piece o' my mind in another article. Your leddyship and the steward hae been pleased to propose that my son Cuddie suld work in the barn wi' a new fangled machine* for dighting the corn frae the chaff, thus impiously thwarting the will of Divine Providence, by raising wind for your leddyship's ain particular use by human art, instead of soliciting it by prayer, or waiting patiently for whatever dispensation of wind Providence was pleased to send upon the sheeling-hill. Now, my leddy'——

* Probably something similar to the barn-fanners now used for winnowing corn, which were not, however, used in their present shape until about 1730. They were objected to by the more rigid sectaries on their first introduction, upon such reasoning as that of honest Mause, in the text,

'The woman would drive ony reasonable being daft!' said Lady Margaret; then, resuming
her tone of authority and indifference, she concluded, 'Weel, Mause, I'll just end where I suld
have began——ye're ower learned and ower godly
for me to dispute wi'; sae I have just this to say,
either Cuddie must attend musters when he's
lawfully warned by the ground-officer, or the
sooner him and you flit and quit my bounds the
better; there's nae scarcity o' auld wives or
ploughmen; but, if there were, I had rather that
the rigs of Tillietudlem bare naething but windle-
straes and sandy-lavrocks than they were ploughed by rebels to the king.'

'Aweel, my leddy,' said Mause, 'I was born
here, and thought to die where my father died;
and your leddyship has been a kind mistress, I'll
ne'er deny that, and I'se ne'er cease to pray for
ye, and for Miss Edith, and that ye may be
brought to see the error of your ways.   But
still'——

'The error of my ways,' interrupted Lady
Margaret—'.The error of *my* ways, ye uncivil
woman?'

'Ou ay, my leddy, we are blinded that live in
this valley of tears and darkness, and hae a' ower
mony errors, grit folks as weel as sma'——but, as
I said, my puir benison will rest wi' you and
yours wherever I am.   I will be wae to hear o'
your affliction, and blythe to hear o' your pros-
perity, temporal and spiritual.   But I canna prefer the commands of an earthly mistress to those
of a heavenly master, and sae I am e'en ready to
suffer for righteousness' sake.'

'It is very well,' said Lady Margaret, turning her back in great displeasure; 'ye ken my will, Mause, in the matter. I'll hae nae whiggery in the barony of Tillietudlem—the next thing wad be to set up a conventicle in my very withdrawing room.'

Having said this, she departed with an air of great dignity; and Mause, giving way to feelings which she had suppressed during the interview, —for she, like her mistress had her own feeling of pride,—now lifted up her voice and wept aloud.

Cuddie, whose malady, real or pretended, still detained him in bed, lay perdue during all this conference, snugly ensconced within his boarded bedstead, and terrified to death lest Lady Margaret, whom he held in hereditary reverence, should have detected his presence, and bestowed on him personally some of those bitter reproaches with which she loaded his mother. As soon as he thought her ladyship fairly out of hearing, he bounced up in his nest.

'The foul fa' ye, that I suld say sae,' he cried out to his mother, 'for a lang-tongued wife, as my father, honest man, aye ca'd ye! Couldna ye let the leddy alane wi' your whiggery? And I was e'en as great a gomeril to let ye persuade me to lie up here amang the blankets like a hurcheon, instead o' gaun to the wappen-schaw like other folk. Odd, but I pat a trick on ye, for I was out at the window-bole when your auld back was turned, and awa' down by to hae a baff at the popinjay, and I shot within twa on't. I cheated the leddy for your clavers, but I wasna gaun cheat my joe. But she may marry whae she likes now, for I'm clean dung ower. This is a waur dirdum than we got frae Mr. Gudyill when ye garr'd me refuse to eat the plum-parridge on Yule-eve, as if it were ony matter to God or man whether a pleughman had suppit on minched pies or sour sowens.'

' O, whisht, my bairn, whisht,' replied Mause; ' thou kens nae about thae things—It was forbidden meat, things dedicated to set days and holidays, which are inhibited to the use of protestant Christians.'

' And now,' continued her son, ' ye hae brought the leddy hersel on our hands!—An' I could but hae gotten some decent claes on, I wad hae spanged out o' bed, and tauld her I wad ride where she liked, night or day, an' she wad but leave us the free house and the yaird that grew the best early kale in the hail country, and the cow's grass.'

' O wow! my winsome bairn, Cuddie,' continued the old dame, ' murmur not at the dispensation; never grudge suffering in the gude cause.'

' But what ken I if the cause is gude or no, mither,' rejoined Cuddie, ' for a' ye bleeze out sae muckle doctrine about it? It's clean beyond my comprehension a' thegither. I see nae sae muckle difference atween the twa ways o't as a' the folk pretend. It's very true the curates read aye the same words ower again; and if they be right words, what for no? A gude tale's no the waur o' being twice tauld, I trow; and a body has aye the better chance to understand it. Every body's no sae gleg at the uptake as ye are yoursel, mither.'

'O, my dear Cuddie, this is the sairest distress of a'——O, how often have I shewn ye the difference between a pure evangelical doctrine and ane that's corrupt wi' human inventions? O, my bairn, if no for your ain saul's sake, yet for my gray hairs'——

'Weel, mither,' said Cuddie, interrupting her, 'what need ye mak sae muckle din about it? I hae aye dune whate'er ye bade me, and gaed to kirk whare'er ye likit on the Sundays, and fended weel for you in the ilka days besides. And that's what vexes me mair than a' the rest, when I think how I am to fend for you now in thae brickle times. I am no clear if I can pleugh ony place but the Mains and Mucklewhame, at least I never tried ony other grund, and it wadna come natural to me. And nae neighbouring heritors daur tak us after being turned aff thae bounds for non-enormity.'

'Non-conformity, hinnie,' sighed Mause, 'is the name that thae warldly men gi'e us.'

'Weel, aweel—we'll hae to gang to a far country, may be twall or fifteen miles aff. I could be a dragoon, nae doubt, I can ride and play wi' the broadsword a bit, but ye wad be roaring about your blessing and your gray hairs. (Here Mause's exclamations became extreme.) 'Weel, weel, I but spoke o't; besides ye're ower auld to be sitting cocked up on a baggage-wagon wi' Eppie Dumblane the corporal's wife. Sae what's to come o' us I canna weel see—I doubt I'll hae to tak the hills wi' the wild whigs, as they ca' them, and

then it will be my lot to be shot down like a mawkin at some dykeside, or to be sent to Heaven wi'
a Saint Johnstone's tippit about my hause.'

' O, my bonnie Cuddie, forbear sic carnal, self-
seeking language, whilk is just a misdoubting o'
Providence—I have not seen the son of the righteous begging his bread; sae says the text; and
your father was a douce honest man, though somewhat warldly in his dealings, and cumbered about
earthly things, e'en like yoursel, my jo!'

' Aweel,' said Cuddie, after a little consideration,' I see but ae gate for't, and that's a cauld
coal to blaw at, mither. Howsomever, mither, ye
hae some guess o' a wee bit kindness that's atween Miss Edith and young Mr. Harry Morton, that suld be ca'd young Milnwood, and that
I hae whiles carried a bit book or maybe a bit letter quietly atween them, and made believe never
to ken wha it cam frae, though I keen'd brawly.
There's whiles convenience in looking a wee stupid—and I hae aften seen them walking at e'en
on the little path by Dinglewood-burn; but naebody ever kenn'd a word about it frae Cuddie; I
ken I'm gay thick in the head, but I'm as honest
as our auld fore-hand ox, puir fallow, that I'll
ne'er work ony mair—I hope they'll be as kind to
him that come ahint me as I hae been.—But, as
I was saying, we'll awa down to Milnwood and
tell Mr. Harry our distress. They want a pleughman, and the grund's no unlike our ain—I am
sure Mr. Harry will stand my part, for he's a
kind-hearted gentleman.—I'll get but little penny-
fee, for his uncle, auld Nippie Milnwood, has as
close a grip as the de'il himself. But we'll aye get

a bit bread, and a drap kale, and a fire-side, and theeking ower our heads, and that's a' we'll want for a season—Sae get up, mither, and sort your things to gang away, for, since sae it is that gang we maun, I wad like ill to wait till Mr. Harrison and auld Gudyill cam to pu' us out by the lug and the horn.'

CHAPTER VIII.

The devil a puritan, or any thing else, he is, but a time-server.   *Twelfth Night.*

IT was evening when Mr. Harry Morton perceived an old woman, wrapped in her tartan plaid, supported by a stout, stupid-looking fellow, in hoddin-gray, approach the house of Milnwood. Old Mause made her courtesy, but Cuddie took the lead in addressing Morton. Indeed he had previously stipulated with his mother that he was to manage matters his own way; for though he readily allowed his general inferiority of understanding, and submitted to the guidance of his mother on most ordinary occasions, yet he said, ' For getting a service or getting forward in the warld, he could somegate gar the wee pickle sense he had gang muckle farther than hers, though she could crack like ony minister o' them a.'

Accordingly he thus opened the conversation with young Morton:—

' A braw night this for the rye, your honour; the west park will be bearing bravely this e'en.'

' I do not doubt it, Cuddie; but what can have brought your mother—this is your mother, is it not?' (Cuddie nodded.) ' What can have brought your mother and you down the water so late?'

' Troth, stir, just what gars the auld wives trot —neshessity, stir—I'm seeking for service, stir.'

' For service, Cuddie, and at this time of the year? how comes that?'

Mause could forbear no longer. Proud alike of her cause and her sufferings, she commenced with an affected humility of tone, ' It has pleased Heaven, an' it like your honour, to distinguish us by a visitation.'—

' De'ils in the wife and nae gude!' whispered Cuddie to his mother; ' an ye come out wi' your whiggery, they'll no daur open a door to us through the hail country!' Then aloud and addressing Morton, ' My mother's auld, stir, and she has rather forgotten herself in speaking to my leddy, that canna weel bide to be contradickit, (as I ken naebody likes it if they could help themsels,) especially by her ain folk,—and Mr. Harrison the steward, and Gudyill the butler, they're no very fond o' us, and it's ill sitting at Rome and striving wi' the Pope, sae I thought it best to flit before ill came to waur—and here's a wee bit line to your honour frae a friend will maybe say some mair about it.'

Morton took the billet, and crimsoning up to the ears between joy and surprise, read these words; ' If you can serve these poor helpless people, you will oblige E. B.'

It was a few instants before he could attain composure enough to ask, ' And what is your object, Cuddie? and how can I be of use to you?'

' Wark, stir, wark, and a service, is my object —a bit beild for my mither and mysel—we hae gude plenishing o' our ain, if we had the cast o' a cart to bring it down—and milk and meal, and greens enow, for I'm gay gleg at meal time, and sae is my mother, lang may it be sae—And, for the penny-fee and a' that, I'll just leave it to the laird and you. I ken ye'll no see a poor lad wranged, if ye can help it.'

Morton shook his head. ' For the meat and lodging, Cuddie, I think I can promise something, but the penny-fee will be a hard chapter, I doubt.'

' I'll tak my chance o't, stir, rather than gang down about Hamilton, or ony sic far country.'

' Well, step into the kitchen, Cuddie, and I'll do what I can for you.'

The negociation was not without difficulties. Morton had first to bring over the housekeeper, who made a thousand objections, as usual, in order to have the pleasure of being besought and entreated; but, when she was gained over, it was comparatively easy, to induce old Milnwood to accept of a servant, whose wages were to be in his own option. An out-house was, therefore, assigned to Mause and her son for their habitation, and it was settled that they were for the time to be admitted to eat of the frugal provisions provided for the family until their own establishment should be completed. As for Morton, he exhausted his own very slender stock of money in order to make Cuddie such a present, under the name of *arles*, as might show the sense of the value of the recommendation delivered to him.

'And now we're settled ance mair,' said Cuddie to his mother, 'and if we're no sae bien and comfortable as we were up yonder, yet life's life ony gate, and we're wi' decent kirk-ganging folk o' your ain persuasion, mither; there will be nae quarrelling about that.'

'Of my persuasion, hinnie! waes me for thy blindness and theirs. O, Cuddie, they are but in the court of the Gentiles, and will ne'er win farther ben, I doubt; they are but little better than the prelatists themsels. They wait on the ministry of that blinded man, Peter Poundtext, ance a precious teacher of the Word, but now a backsliding pastor, that has, for the sake of stipend and family maintenance, forsaken the strict path and gone astray after the Black Indulgence. O, my son, had ye but profited by the gospel doctrines ye hae heard in the Glen o' Bengonnar from the dear Richard Rumbleberry, that sweet youth, wha suffered martyrdom in the Grassmarket, afore Candlemas! Didna ye hear him say, that Erastianism was as bad as prelacy, and that the Indulgence was as bad as Erastianism?'

'Heard ever ony body the like o' this,' interrupted Cuddie, 'we'll be driven out o' house and ha' again afore we ken where to turn oursels. Weel, mither, I hae just ae word mair—An' I hear ony mair o' your din—afore folk, that is, for I dinna mind your clavers mysel, they aye set me sleeping—but if I hear ony mair din afore folk, as I was saying, about Poundtexts and Rumbleberries, and doctrines and malignants, I'se e'en turn a single sodger mysel, or maybe a serjeant or a captain if ye plague me the mair, and let

Rumbleberry and you gang to the de'il thegither.
I ne'er gat ony gude by his doctrine, as ye ca't,
but a gude fit o' the batts wi' sitting amang the
wat moss-hags for four hours at a yoking, and the
leddy cured me wi' some hickery-pickery, mair
by token, an' she had kenn'd how I came by the
disorder, she wadna hae been in sic a hurry to
cure it.'

Although groaning in spirit over the obdurate
and impenitent state, as she thought it, of her son
Cuddie, Mause durst neither urge him farther on
the topic, nor altogether neglect the warning he
had given her. She knew the disposition of her
deceased helpmate, whom this surviving pledge
of their union greatly resembled, and remembered, that although submitting implicitly in most
things to her boast of superior acuteness, he used
on certain occasions when driven to extremity, to
be seized with fits of obstinacy which neither re-
monstrance, flattery, nor threats, were capable of
overpowering. Trembling, therefore, at the very
possibility of Cuddie's fulfilling his threat, she put
a guard over her tongue, and even when Poundtext was commended in her presence, as an able
and fructifying preacher, she had the good sense
to suppress the contradiction which thrilled upon
her tongue, and to express her sentiments no
otherwise than by deep groans, which the hearers
charitably construed to flow from a vivid recollection of the more pathetic parts of his homilies.
How long she could have repressed her feelings it
is difficult to say. An unexpected accident relieved her from the necessity.

The Laird of Milnwood kept up all old fashions which were connected with economy. It was, therefore, still the custom in his house, as it had been universal in Scotland about fifty years before, that the domestics, after having placed the dinner on the table, sate down at the lower end of the board, and partook of the share which was assigned to them, in company with their masters. Upon the day, therefore, after Cuddie's arrival, being the third from the opening of this narrative, old Robin, who was butler, valet-de-chambre, footman, gardener, and what not, in the house of Milnwood, placed on the table an immense charger of broth, thickened with oatmeal and colewort, in which ocean of liquid was indistinctly discovered, by close observers, two or three short ribs of lean mutton sailing to and fro. Two huge baskets, one of bread made of barley and pease, and one of oat-cakes, flanked this standing dish. A large boiled salmon would now-a-days have indicated more liberal housekeeping; but at that period it was caught in such plenty in the considerable rivers in Scotland, that it was generally applied to feed the servants, who are said sometimes to have stipulated that they should not be required to eat a food so luscious and surfeiting in its quality above five times a-week. The large black-jack, filled with very small beer of Milnwood's own brewing, was indulged to the servants at discretion, as were the bannocks, cakes, and broth; but the mutton was reserved for the heads of the family, Mrs. Wilson included; and a measure of ale, somewhat deserving the name, was set apart in a silver tankard for their exclusive use. A huge kebbock, (a cheese that is made with ewe milk mixed with cow's milk) and a jar of salt butter, were in common to the company.

To enjoy this exquisite cheer, was placed at the head of the table the old laird himself, with his nephew on the one side, and the favourite house-keeper on the other. At a long interval, and beneath the salt of course, sate old Robin, a meagre, half-starved serving-man, rendered cross and cripple by the rheumatism, and a dirty drab of a house-maid, whom use had rendered callous to the daily exercitations which her temper underwent at the hands of her master and Mrs. Wilson. A barn-man, a white-headed cow-herd boy, and Cuddie the new ploughman and his mother, completed the party. The other labourers belonging to the property resided in their own houses, happy at least in this, that if their cheer was not more delicate than that which we have described, they could at least eat their fill, unwatched by the sharp, envious, gray eyes of Milnwood, which seemed to measure the quantity that each of his dependants swallowed, as closely as if their glances attended each mouthful in its progress from the lips to the stomach. This close inspection was unfavourable to Cuddie, who was much prejudiced in his new master's opinion, by the silent celerity with which he caused the victuals to disappear before him. And ever and anon Milnwood turned his eyes from the huge feeder to cast indignant glances upon his nephew, whose repugnance to rustic labour was the principal cause of his needing a ploughman, and who had been the direct means of his hiring this very cormorant.

'Pay thee wages, quotha?' said Milnwood to himself. 'Thou wilt eat in a week the value of mair than thou canst work for in a month.'

These disagreeable ruminations were interrupted by a loud knocking at the outergate. It was a universal custom in Scotland, that, when the family was at dinner, the outer-gate of the courtyard, if there was one, and, if not, the door of the house itself, was always shut and locked, and only guests of importance, or persons upon urgent business, sought or received admittance at that time. The family of Milnwood were therefore surprised, and, in the unsettled state of the times, some thing alarmed, at the earnest and repeated knocking with which the gate was now assailed. Mrs. Wilson ran in person to the door, and, having reconnoitered those who were so clamorous for admittance, through some secret aperture with which most Scotish door-ways were furnished for the express purpose, she returned wringing her hands in great dismay, exclaiming, 'The red-coats! the red-coats!'

'Robin——Ploughman——What ca' they ye?—— Barnsman——Nevoy Harry——open the door, open the door,' exclaimed old Milnwood, snatching up and slipping into his pocket the two or three silver spoons with which the upper end of the table was garnished, those beneath the salt being of goodly horn. 'Speak them fair, sirs—Lord love ye, speak them fair—they winna bide thrawing— we're a' harried—we're a' harried!'

While the servants admitted the troopers, whose oaths and threats already indicated resentment at the delay they had been put to, Cuddie

took the opportunity to whisper to his mother,
' Now, ye daft auld carline, mak yoursel deaf—
ye hae made us a' deaf ere now—and let me speak
for ye. I wad like ill to get my neck raxed for an
auld wife's clashes, though ye be our mither.'

' O, hinny, ay; I'se be silent or thou sall come
to ill,' was the corresponding whisper of Mause;
' but bethink ye, my dear, them that deny the
Word, the Word will deny.'—

Her admonition was cut short by the entrance
of the Life Guard's-men, a party of four troopers
commanded by Bothwell.

In they tramped, making a tremendous clatter
upon the stone floor with the iron-shod heels of
their large jack-boots, and the clash and clang of
their long, heavy, basket-hilted broadswords.
Milnwood and his housekeeper trembled, from
well-grounded apprehension of the system of ex-
action and plunder carried on during these domi-
ciliary visits. Henry Morton was discomposed
with more special cause, for he remembered that
he stood answerable to the laws for having har-
boured Burley. The widow Mause Headrigg,
between fear for her son's life and an over-strain-
ed and enthusiastic zeal, which reproached her
for consenting even tacitly to belie her religious
sentiments, was in a strange quandary. The other
servants quaked for they knew not well what.
Cuddie alone, with the look of supreme indifference and stupidity which a Scotish peasant can
at times assume as a masque for considerable
shrewdness and craft, continued to swallow large
spoonfuls of his broth, to command which, he had
drawn within his sphere the large vessel that con-

tained it, and helped himself, amid the confusion, to a sevenfold portion.

' What is your pleasure here, gentlemen?' said Milnwood, humbling himself before the satellites of power.

' We come in behalf of the king,' answered Bothwell; ' Why the devil did you keep us so long standing at the door?'

' We were at dinner,' answered Milnwood, ' and the door was locked, as is usual in landward towns in this country. I am sure, gentlemen, if I had kenn'd ony servants of our gude king had stood at the door—But wad ye please to drink some ale—or some brandy—or a cup of canary sack, or claret wine?' making a pause between each offer as long as a stingy bidder at an auction, who is loth to advance his offer for a favourite lot.

' Claret for me,' said one fellow.

' I like ale better,' said another, ' provided it is right juice of John Barleycorn.'

' Better never was malted,' said Milnwood; ' I can hardly say sae muckle for the claret. It's thin and cauld, gentlemen.'

' Brandy will cure that,' said a third fellow; ' a glass of brandy to three glasses of wine prevents the curmurring in the stomach.'

' Brandy, ale, wine, sack, and claret,—we'll try them all,' said Bothwell, ' and stick to that which is best. There's good sense in that, if the damn'd-est whig in Scotland had said it.'

Hastily, yet with a reluctant quiver of his muscles, Milnwood lugged out two ponderous keys, and delivered them to the governante.

'The housekeeper,' said Bothwell, taking a seat, and throwing himself upon it, 'is neither so young nor so bonny as to tempt a man to follow her to the gauntrees, and devil a one here is there worth sending in her place.——What's this?—— meat?' (searching with a fork among the broth, and fishing up a cutlet of mutton)—'I think I could eat a bit—it's as tough as if the devil's dam had hatched it.'

'If there is any thing better in the house, sir,' said Milnwood, alarmed at these symptoms of disapprobation——

'No, no,' said Bothwell, 'it's not worth while, I must proceed to business.——You attend Pound-text, the presbyterian parson, I understand, Mr. Morton?'

Mr. Morton hastened to slide in a confession and apology.

'By the indulgence of his gracious majesty and the government, for I wad do nothing out of law —I hae nae objection whatever to the establish-ment of a moderate episcopacy, but only that I am a country-bred man, and the ministers are a hamelier kind of folk, and I can follow their doc-trine better; and, with reverence, sir, it's a mair frugal establishment for the country.'

'Well, I care nothing about that,' said Both-well; 'they are indulged, and there's an end of it; but, for my part, if I were to give the law, never a crop-eared cur of the whole pack should bark in a Scotch pulpit. However, I am to obey com-mands. There comes the liquor; put it down, my good old lady.'

He decanted about one half of a quart bottle of claret into a wooden quaigh or bicker, and took it off at a draught.

'You did your good wine injustice, my friend; —it's better than your brandy, though that's good too. Will you pledge me to the king's health?'

'With pleasure,' said Milnwood, ' in ale,—but I never drink claret, and keep only a very little for some honoured friends.'

'Like me, I suppose,' said Bothwell; and then, pushing the bottle to Henry, he said, 'Here, young man, pledge you the king's health.'

Henry filled a moderate glass in silence, regardless of the hints and pushes of his uncle, which seemed to indicate that he ought to have followed his example in preferring beer to wine.

'Well,' said Bothwell, 'have ye all drank the toast?—What is that old wife about? Give her a glass of brandy, she shall drink the king's health, by'——

'If your honour pleases,' said Cuddie, with great stolidity of aspect, ' this is my mither, stir; and she's as deaf as Corralinn; we canna make her hear day nor door; but, if your honour pleases, I am ready to drink the king's health for her in as mony glasses of brandy as ye think neshessary.'

'I dare swear you are,' answered Bothwell, 'you look like a fellow that would stick to brandy —help thyself, man; all's free where'er I come.— Tom, help the maid to a comfortable cup, though she's but a dirty jilt neither. Fill round once more—Here's to our noble commander, Colonel Graham of Claverhouse!—What the devil is the old woman groaning for? She looks as very a whig as ever sate on a hill side—Do you renounce the Covenant, good woman?'

' Whilk Covenant is your honour meaning? Is it the Covenant of Works, or the Covenant of Grace?' said Cuddie, interposing.

' Any covenant, all covenants that ever were hatched,' answered the trooper.

' Mither,' cried Cuddie, affecting to speak as to a deaf person, ' the gentleman wants to ken if ye will renunce the Covenant of Works.'

' With all my heart, Cuddie,' said Mause, ' and pray that my feet may be delivered from the snare thereof.'

' Come,' said Bothwell,' the old dame has come more frankly off than I expected. Another cup round, and then we'll proceed to business.—You have all heard, I suppose, of the horrid and barbarous murder committed upon the person of the Archbishop of St. Andrews, by ten or eleven armed fanatics?'

All started and looked at each other; at length Milnwood himself answered, ' They had heard of some such misfortune, but were in hopes it had not been true.'

' There is the relation published by government, old gentleman; what do you think of it?'

' Think, sir? Wh—wh—whatever the council please to think of it,' stammered Milnwood.

' I desire to have your opinion more explicitly, my friend,' said the dragoon authoritatively.

Milnwood's eyes hastily glanced through the paper to pick out the strongest expressions of censure with which it abounded, in gleaning

which he was greatly aided by their being print-
ed in italics!

'I think it a—bloody and execrable—murder
and parricide—devised by hellish and implacable
cruelty—utterly abominable, and a scandal to the
land.'

'Well said, old gentleman,' said the querist—
'Here's to thee, and I wish you joy of your good
principles. You owe me a cup of thanks for
having taught you them; nay, thou shalt pledge
me in thine own sack—sour ale sits ill upon a
loyal stomach——Now comes your turn, young
man; what think you of the matter in hand?'

'I should have little objection to answer you,'
said Henry, 'if I knew what right you had to put
the question.'

'The Lord preserve us!' said the old housekeeper, 'to ask the like o' that at a trooper, when
a' folk ken they do whatever they like through
the hail country wi' man and woman, beast and
body.'

The old gentleman exclaimed in the same horror at his nephew's audacity. 'Hold your peace,
sir, or answer the gentleman discreetly. Do you
mean to affront the king's authority in the person
of a serjeant of the life-guards?'

'Silence, all of you, exclaimed Bothwell, striking his hand fiercely on the table,—'Silence,
every one of you, and hear me!—You ask me for
my right to examine you, sir; (to Henry) my
cockade and my broadsword are my commission,
and a better one than ever Old Nol gave to his
round-heads; and if you want to know more
about it, you may look at the act of council em-

powering his majesty's officers and soldiers to search for, examine, and apprehend suspicious persons; and, therefore, once more, I ask you your opinion of the death of Archbishop Sharpe —it's a new touchstone we have got for trying people's metal.'

Henry had, by this time, reflected upon the useless risk to which he would expose the family by resisting the tyrannical power which was delegated to such rude hands; he therefore read the narrative over, and replied, composedly, ' I have no hesitation to say, that the perpetrators of this assassination have committed, in my opinion, a rash and wicked action, which I regret the more, as I foresee it will be made the cause of proceedings against many who are both innocent of the deed, and as far from approving it as myself.'

While Henry thus expressed himself, Bothwell, who bent his eyes keenly upon him, seemed suddenly to recollect his features.

' Aha! my friend Captain Popinjay, I think I have seen you before, and in very suspicious company.'

' I saw you once,' answered Henry, ' in the public-house of the town of ——'

' And with whom did you leave that public-house, youngster?—Was it not with John Balfour of Burley, one of the murderers of the Archbishop?'

' I did leave the house with the person you have named,' answered Henry, ' I scorn to deny it; but, so far from knowing him to be a murderer of the primate, I did not even know at the time that such a crime had been committed.'

'Lord have mercy on me, I am ruined!—utterly ruined and undone!' exclaimed Milnwood. 'That callant's tongue will rin the head aff his ain shoulders, and waste my gudes to the very gray cloak on my back.'

'But you know Burley,' continued Bothwell, still addressing Henry, and regardless of his uncle's interruption, 'to be an intercommuned rebel and traitor, and you knew the prohibition to deal with such persons. You knew, that, as a loyal subject, you were prohibited to reset, supply, or intercommune with this attainted traitor, to correspond with him by word, writ, or message, or to supply him with meat, drink, house, harbour, or victual, under the highest pains—You knew all this, and yet you broke the law.' (Henry was silent.) 'Where did you part from him?' continued Bothwell; 'was it in the highway, or did you give him harbourage in this very house?'

'In this house!' said his uncle, 'he dared not for his neck bring ony traitor into a house of mine.'

'Dare he deny that he did so?' said Bothwell.

'As you charge it to me as a crime,' said Henry, 'you will excuse my saying any thing that will criminate myself.'

'O, the lands of Milnwood!—the bonny lands of Milnwood, that have been in the name of Morton twa hundred years!' exclaimed his uncle; they are barking and fleeing, outfield and infield, haugh and holme!'

'No, sir,' said Henry, 'you shall not suffer on my account—I own,' he continued, addressing

Bothwell, ' I did give this man a night's lodging, as to an old military comrade of my father. But it was not only without my uncle's knowledge, but contrary to his express general orders. I trust, if my evidence is considered as good against myself, it will have some weight in proving my uncle's innocence.'

' Come, young man,' said the soldier, in a somewhat milder tone, ' you're a smart spark enough, and I am sorry for you; and your uncle here is a fine old Trojan, kinder, I see, to his guests than himself, for he gives us wine and drinks his own thin ale—tell me all you know about this Burley, what he said when you parted from him, where he went, and where he is likely now to be found; and d——n it, I'll wink as hard on your share of the business as my duty will permit. There's a thousand merks on the murdering whigamore's head, an' I could but light on it—Come, out with it—where did you part with him?'

' You will excuse my answering that question, sir,' said Morton; ' the same cogent reasons which induced me to afford him hospitality at considerable risk to myself and my friends, would command me to respect his secret, if indeed he had trusted me with any.'

' So you refuse to give me an answer?' said Bothwell.

' I have none to give,' returned Henry.

' Perhaps I could teach you to find one, by tying a piece of lighted match betwixt your fingers,' answered Bothwell.

'O, for pity's sake, sir,' said old Alison apart to her master, ' gi'e them siller—it's siller they're seeking—they'll murder Mr. Henry, and yoursel next.'

Milnwood groaned in perplexity and bitterness of spirit, and with a tone as if he was giving up the ghost, exclaimed, ' If twenty p—p—punds would make up this unhappy matter'——

' My master,' insinuated Alison to the serjeant, ' would gi'e twenty punds sterling.'

' Punds Scotch, you b—h,' interrupted Milnwood, for the agony of his avarice overcame alike his puritanic precision and the habitual respect he entertained for his housekeeper.

' Punds sterling,' insisted the housekeeper, ' if ye wad hae the gudeness to look ower the lad's misconduct; he's that dour ye might tear him to pieces, and ye wad ne'er get a word out o' him; and it wad do ye little gude to burn his bonny finger ends.'

' Why,' said Bothwell, hesitating, ' I don't know—most of my cloth would have the money, and take off the prisoner too; but I bear a conscience, and if your master will stand to your offer, and enter into bond to produce his nephew, and if all in the house will take the test-oath, I do not know but'——

' O ay, ay, sir,' cried Mrs. Wilson, ' ony test, ony oaths ye please!' And then aside to her master, ' Haste ye away, sir, and get the money, or they will burn the house about our lugs.'

Old Milnwood cast a rueful look upon his adviser, and moved off, like a piece of Dutch clock-work, to set at liberty his imprisoned angels in this dire emergency. Meanwhile, Serjeant Bothwell began to put the test-oath with such a degree of solemn reverence as might have been expected, being just about the same which is used to this day in his majesty's custom-house.

' You—what's your name, woman?'

' Alison Wilson, sir.'

' You, Alison Wilson, solemnly swear, certify, and declare, that you judge it unlawful for subjects under pretext of reformation, or any other pretext whatsoever, to enter into Leagues and Covenants'——

Here the ceremony was interrupted by a strife between Cuddie and his mother, which, long conducted in whispers, now became audible.

' O, whisht, mither, whisht! they're upon a communing—Oh! whisht, and they'll agree weel e'enow.'

' I will not whisht, Cuddie,' replied his mother. ' I will uplift my voice and spare not—I will confound the man of sin, even the scarlet man, and through my voice shall Mr. Henry be freed from the net of the fowler.'

' She has her leg ower the harrows now,' said Cnddie, ' stop her wha can—I see her cocked up behint a dragoon on her way to the Tolbooth—I find my ain legs tied below a horse's belly—Ay —she has just mustered up her sermon, and there—wi' that grane—out it comes, and we are a' ruined, horse and foot!'

' And div ye think to come here,' said Mause, her whithered hand shaking in concert with her keen, though wrinkled visage, animated by zealous wrath, and emancipated by the very mention

of the test, from the restraints of her own prudence and Cuddie's admonition—'div ye think
to come here, wi' your soul-killing, saint-seduc-
ing, conscience-confounding oaths, and tests, and
bands—your snares, and your traps, and your
gins?—Surely it is in vain that a net is spread in
the sight of any bird.'

'Eh! what, good dame?' said the soldier.
'Here's a whig miracle, egad! the old wife has
got both her ears and tongue, and we are like to
be driven deaf in our turn.—Go to, hold your
peace, and remember whom you talk to, you old
idiot.'

'Whae do I talk to? Eh, sirs, ower weel may
the sorrowing land ken what ye are. Malignant
adherents ye are to the prelates, foul props to a
feeble and filthy cause, bloody beasts of prey,
and burdens to the earth.'

'Upon my soul,' said Bothwell, astonished as
a mastiff-dog might be should a hen-partridge fly
at him in defence of her young, 'this is the finest
language I ever heard! Can't you give us some
more of it?'

'Gi'e ye some mair o't?' said Mause, clearing
her voice with a preliminary cough, 'I will take
up my testimony against you ance and again.—
Philistines ye are, and Edomites—leopards are
ye, and foxes—evening-wolves, that gnaw not the
bones till the morrow—wicked dogs, that compass about the chosen—thrusting kine, and pushing bulls of Bashan—piercing serpents ye are, and
allied baith in name and nature with the great
Red Dragon, Revelations, twalfth chapter, third
and fourth verses.'

Here the old lady stopped, apparently much more from lack of breath than of matter.

'Curse the old hag,' said one of the dragoons, 'gag her, and take her to head-quarters.'

'For shame, Andrews,' said Bothwell; 're-member the good lady belongs to the fair sex, and uses only the privilege of her tongue.——But, hark ye, good woman, every Bull of Bashan and Red Dragon will not be so civil as I am, or be contented to leave you to the charge of the con-stable and ducking-stool. In the mean time, I must necessarily carry off this young man to head-quarters. I cannot answer to my commanding-officer to leave him in a house where I have heard so much treason and fanaticism.'

'See now, mither, what ye hae dune,' whisper-ed Cuddie; 'there's the Philistines, as ye ca' them, are gaun to whirry awa' Mr. Harry, and a' wi' your nash-gab, de'il be on't!'

'Haud ye're tongue, ye cowardly loon, said the mother, 'and lay na the wyte on me; if you and thae thowless gluttons that are sitting staring like cows bursting on clover, wad testify wi' your hands as I have testified wi' my tongue, they should never harle the precious young lad awa' to captivity.

While this dialogue passed, the soldiers had already bound and secured their prisoner. Miln-wood returned at this instant, and, alarmed at the preparations he beheld, hastened to proffer to Bothwell, though with many a grievous groan, the purse of gold which he had been obliged to rummage out as ransom for his nephew. The trooper took the purse with an air of indifference, weighed it in his hand, chucked it up into the air, and caught it as it fell, then shook his head, and said, ' There's many a merry night in this nest of yellow boys, but d——n me if I dare venture for them—that old woman has spoke too loud, and before all the men too.——Hark ye, old gentleman,' to Milnwood, ' I must take your nephew to head-quarters, so I cannot, in conscience, keep more than is my due as civility-money;' then, opening the purse, he gave a gold piece to each of the soldiers, and took three to himself; ' Now,' said he, ' you have the comfort to know that your kinsman, young captain Popinjay, will be carefully looked after and civilly used, and the rest of the money I return to you.'

Milnwood eagerly extended his hand.

' Only you know,' said Bothwell, still playing with the purse, ' that every land-holder is answerable for the conformity and loyalty of his household, and that these fellows of mine are not obliged to be silent on the subject of the fine sermon we have had from that old puritan in the tartan -plaid there; and I presume you are aware that the consequences of delation will be a heavy fine before the council.'

' Good serjeant,—worthy captain!' exclaimed the terrified miser, ' I am sure there is no person in my house, to my knowledge, would give cause of offence.'

' Nay,' answered Bothwell, ' you shall hear her give her testimony, as she calls it, herself.——You fellow,' (to Cuddie) ' stand back and let your mother speak her mind. I see she's primed and loaded again since her first discharge.'

' Lord! noble sir,' said Cuddie, ' an auld wife's tongue's but a feckless matter to mak sic a fash about. Neither my father nor me ever minded muckle what our mither said.'

' Hold your peace, my lad, while you are well,' said Bothwell; ' I promise you I think you are slyer than you would like to be supposed.—Come, good dame, you see your master will not believe that you can give us so bright a testimony.'

Mause's zeal did not require this spur to set her again on full career.

' Wo to the compliers and carnal self-seekers,' she said, ' that daubs over and drowns their con- sciences by complying with wicked exactions, and giving mammon of unrighteousness to the sons of Belial, that it may make their peace with them! It is a sinful compliance, a base confederacy with the enemy. It is the evil that Menahan did in the sight of the Lord, when he gave a thousand talents to Peel, King of Assyria, that his hand might be with him, Second Kings, feifteen chap- ter, aughteen verse. It is the evil deed of Ahab, when he sent money to Tigteth Peleaser, see the same, Second Kings, saxteen and aught. And if it was accounted a backsliding even in godly Hezekiah, that he complied with Sennacherib, giving him money and offering to bear that which was put upon him, (see the saame Second Kings, aughteen chapter, fourteen and feifteen verses) even so it is with them that in this contumacious and backsliding generation pays localities and fees, and cess and fines, to greedy and unrighteous publicans, and extortions and stipends to hireling curates, (dumb dogs which bark not, sleeping, lying down, loving to slumber) and gives gifts to be helps and hires to our oppressors and destroyers. They are all like the castors of a lot with them—like the preparing of a table for the troop, and the furnishing a drink-offering to the number.'

' There's a fine sound of doctrine for you, Mr. Morton! How like you that?' said Bothwell; ' or how do you think the Council will like it? I think we can carry the greatest part of it in our heads without a kylevine pen and a pair of tablets, such as you bring to conventicles. She denies paying cess, I think, Andrews?'

' Yes, by G——,' said Andrews; ' and she swore it was a sin to give a trooper a pot of ale, or ask him to sit down at a table.'

' You hear,' said Bothwell, addressing Milnwood, ' but it's your own affair; and he proffered back the purse with its diminished contents, with an air of indifference.

Milnwood, whose head seemed stunned by the accumulation of his misfortunes, extended his hand mechanically to take the purse.

' Are ye mad?' said his housekeeper, in a whisper; ' tell them to keep it.—They will keep it either by fair means or foul, and it's our only chance to make them quiet.'

' I canna do it, Ailie—I canna do it,' said Milnwood, in the bitterness of his heart. ' I canna part wi' the siller I hae counted sae often ower, to thae blackguards.'

' Then, I maun do it mysel, Milnwood,' said the housekeeper, ' or see a' gang wrang thegither. —My master, sir,' she said, addressing Bothwell,

'canna think o' taking back ony thing at the hand
of an honourable gentleman like you; he implores
ye to pit up the siller, and be as kind to his
nephew as you can, and be favourable in report-
ing our dispositions to government, and let us tak
nae wrang for the daft speeches of an auld jaud,'
(here she turned fiercely upon Mause, to indulge
herself for the effort which it cost her to assume
a mild demeanor to the soldiers,) ' a daft auld
whig randie, that ne'er was in the house (foul fa'
her) till yesterday afternoon, and that sall ne'er
cross the door-stane again an' anes I had her out
o't.'

' Ay, ay,' said Cuddie, ' e'en sae. I kenn'd we
wad be put to our travels again whene'er you
suld get three words spoken to an end. I was
sure that wad be the upshot o't, mither.'

' Whisht, my bairn,' said she, ' and dinna mur
mur at the cross—cross their door-stane! weel I
wot I'll ne'er cross their door-stane. There's
nae mark on their threshold for a signal that the
destroying angel should pass by. They'll get
a back-cast o' his hand yet, that think sae muckle
o' the creature and sae little o' the Creator—sae
muckle o' warld's gear, and sae little o' a broken
covenant—sae muckle about thae wheen pieces
o' yellow muck, and sae little about the pure gold
o' the Scripture—sae muckle about their ain
friend and kinsman, and sae little about the elect
that are tried wi' hornings, harrassings, huntings,
searchings, chasings, catchings, imprisonments,
torturings, banishments, headings, hangings, dis-
memberings, and quarterings quick, forbye the
hundreds forced from their ain habitations to the

deserts, mountains, muirs, mosses, moss-flows, and peat-hags, there to hear the word like bread eaten in secret.'

' She's at the Covenant now, serjent, shall we not have her away?' said one of the soldiers.

' You be d——d,' said Bothwell, aside to him; ' cannot you see she's better where she is so long as there is a respectable, sponsible, money-broking heritor, like Mr. Morton of Milnwood, who has the means of atoning her trespasses? Let the old mother fly to raise another brood, she's too tough to be made any thing of herself——Here,' he cried, ' one other round to Milnwood and his roof-tree, and to our next merry meeting with him!——which I think will be not far distant, if he keeps such a fanatical family.'

' He then ordered the party to take their horses, and pressed the best in Milnwood's stable into the king's service to carry the prisoner. Mrs. Wilson, with weeping eyes, made up a small parcel of necessaries for Henry's compelled journey, and, as she bustled about, took an opportunity, unseen by the party, to slip into his hand a small sum of money. Bothwell and his troopers, in other respects, kept their promise, and were civil. They did not bind their prisoner, but contented themselves with leading his horse between a file of men. They then mounted, and marched off with much mirth and laughter among themselves, leaving the Milnwood family in great confusion. The old laird himself, overpowered by the loss of his nephew, and the unavailing outlay of twenty pounds sterling, did nothing the whole evening but rock himself backwards and forwards in his great leathern easy-chair, repeating the same lamentation, of 'Ruined on a' sides, ruined on a' sides—body and gudes, body and gudes!'

Mrs. Alison Wilson's grief was partly indulged and partly relieved by the torrent of invectives with which she accompanied Mause and Cuddie's expulsion from Milnwood.

'Ill luck be in the graning corse o' thee! the prettiest lad in Clydesdale this day maun be a sufferer, and a' for you and your daft whiggery.'

'Gae wa',' replied Mause; 'I trow ye are yet in the bonds of sin, and in the gall of iniquity, to grudge your bonniest and best in the cause of Him that gave ye a' ye hae—I promise I hae dune as muckle for Mr. Harry as I wad do for my ain; for, if Cuddie was found worthy to bear testimony in the Grassmarket.'———

'And there's gude hope o't,' said Alison, 'unless you and he change your courses.'

'And if,' continued Mause, disregarding the interruption, 'the bloody Doegs and the flattering Ziphites were to seek to insnare me with a proffer of his remission upon sinful compliances, I wad persevere, nathelesss, in lifting my testimony against popery, prelacy, antinomianism, erastianism, lapsarianism, sublapsarianism, and the sins and snares of the times—I wad cry as a woman in labour against the black indulgences, that has been a stumbling-block to professors—I wad uplift my voice as a powerful preacher.'

'Hout tout, mither,' cried Cuddie, interfering, and dragging her off forcibly, 'dinna deave the gentlewoman wi' your testimony; ye hae preached eneugh for sax days; ye preached us out o' our can-

ny free-house and gude kale-yard, and out o'
this new city o' refuge afore our hinder-end was
weel hafted in it; and ye hae preached Mr. Harry awa' to the prison; and ye hae preached twenty punds out o' the laird's pocket that he likes as
ill to quit wi'; and sae ye may haud sae for ae
wee while without preaching me up a ladder and
down a tow; sae cum awa', cum awa';/the family
hae had eneugh o' your testimony to mind it for
ae while.'

So saying he dragged off Mause, the words
' Testimony—Covenant--malignants—indulgence,'
still thrilling upon her tongue, to make preparations for instantly renewing their travels in quest
of an assylum.

' Ill-fa'ard, crazy, crack-brained gowk, that she
is!' exclaimed the housekeeper, as she saw them
depart, ' to set up to be sae muckle better than
ither folk, the ould besom, and to bring sae muckle distress on a douce quiet family! If it hadna
been that I am mair than half a gentlewoman by
my station, I wad hae tried my ten nails in the
wizen'd hide o' her.'

CHAPTER VIII.

I am a son of mars who have been in many wars,
And shew my cuts and scars wherever I come;
This here was for a wench, and that other in a trench,
When welcoming the French at the sound of the drum.

Burns.

' Don't be too much cast down,' said Sergeant
Bothwell to his prisoner as they journeyed on to-

wards the head-quarters; 'you are a smart pretty lad, and well connected; the worst that will happen will be strapping up for it, and that is many an honest fellow's lot. I tell you fairly your life's within the compass of the law, unless you make submission, and get off by a round fine upon your uncle's estate; he can well afford it.'

'That vexes me more than the rest,' said Henry. 'He parts with his money with regret; and, as he had no concern whatever with my having given this person shelter for a night, I wish to Heaven, if I escape capital punishment, that the penalty may be of a kind I could bear in my own person.'

'Why, perhaps,' said Bothwell, 'they will propose to you to go into one of the Scotch regiments that are serving abroad. It's no bad line of service; if your friends are active, and there are any knocks going, you may soon get a commission.'

'I am by no means sure,' answered Morton, 'that such a sentence is not the best thing that can happen to me.'

'Why, then, you are no real whig after all?' said the serjeant.

'I have hitherto meddled with no party in the state,' said Henry, 'but have remained quietly at home: and sometimes I have had serious thoughts of joining one of our foreign regiments.'

'Have you?' replied Bothwell; 'why, I honour you for it; I have served in the Scotch French guards myself many a long day; it's the place for learning discipline, d—n me. They never mind what you do when you are off duty; but miss the roll call, and see how they will arrange you—D—n me, if old Captain Montgomery didn't make me

mount guard upon the arsenal in my steel back and
breast, plate-sleeves and head-piece, for six hours
at once, under so burning a sun, that gad I was
beeked like a turtle in Port Royale. I swore never
to miss answering to Francis Stuart again, though
I should leave my hand of cards upon the drum-
head—Ah! discipline is a capital thing.'

'In other respects you liked the service?' said
Henry.

'*Par excellence*,' said Bothwell, 'women, wine,
and wassail, all to be had for little but the asking;
and if you find it in your conscience to let a fat
priest think he has some chance to convert you,
gad he'll help you to these comforts himself just to
gain a little ground in your good affection. Where
will you find a crop-eared whig parson will be so
civil?'

'Why, nowhere, I agree with you,' said Henry;
'but what was your chief duty?'

'To guard the king's person,' said Bothwell, 'to
look after the safety of Louis le Grand, my boy,
and now and then to take a turn among the Hugue-
nots (protestants that is.) And there we had fine
scope; it brought my hand pretty well in for the
service in this country. But, come, as you are to be
a *buon camerado*, as the Spaniards say, I must put
you in cash with some of your old uncle's broad-
pieces. This is cutter's law; we must not see a pretty fellow want, if we have cash ourselves.'

Thus speaking, he pulled out his purse, took out
some of the contents, and offered them to Henry
without counting them. Young Morton declined
the favour; and, not judging it prudent to acquaint
the serjeant, notwithstanding his apparent generosi-

ty, that he was actually in possession of some money, he assured him he would have no difficulty in getting a supply from his uncle.

' Well,' said Bothwell, ' in that case these yellow rascals must serve to ballast my purse a little longer. I always make it a rule never to quit the tavern (unless ordered on duty) while my purse is so weighty that I can chuck it over the sign-post. When it is so light that the wind blows it back, then, boot and saddle,—we must fall on some way of replenishing.—But what tower is that before us, rising so high upon the steep bank, out of the woods that surround it on every side?'

' It is the tower of Tillietudlem,' said one of the soldiers. ' Old lady Margaret Bellenden lives there. She's one of the best affected women in the country, and one that's a soldier's friend. When I was hurt by one of the d—d whig dogs that shot at me from behind a fauld-dyke, I lay a month there, and would stand such another wound to be in as good quarters again.'

' If that be the case,' said Bothwell, ' I will pay my respects to her as we pass, and request some refreshment for men and horses; I am as thirsty already as if I had drank nothing at Milnwood. But it is a good thing in these times,' he continued, addressing himself to Henry, ' that the king's soldier cannot pass a house without getting a refreshment. In such houses as Tillie—what d'ye call it, you are served for love; in the houses of the avowed fanatics you help yourself by force: and among the moderate presbyterians and other suspicious persons, you are well treated from fear; so your thirst is always quenched on some terms or other.'

'And you propose,' said Henry anxiously, ' to go upon that errand up to the tower yonder?'

'To be sure I do,' answered Bothwell. 'How should I be able to report favourably to my officers of the worthy lady's sound principles, unless I know the taste of her sack, for sack she will produce—that I take for granted; it is the favourite consoler of your old dowager of quality, as small claret is the potation of your country laird.'

'Then, for Heaven's sake,' said Henry, ' if you are determined to go there, do not mention my name, or expose me to a family that I am acquainted with. Let me be muffled up for the time in one of your soldier's cloaks, and only mention me generally as a prisoner under your charge.'

'With all my heart,' said Bothwell; ' I promised to use you civilly, and I scorn to break my word.— Here, Andrews, wrap a cloak round the prisoner, and do not mention his name, nor where we caught him, unless you would have a trot on a horse of wood.'

They were at this moment at an arched gateway, battlemented and flanked with turrets, one whereof was totally ruinous, excepting the lower story, which served as a cow-house to the peasant, whose family inhabited the turret which remained entire. The gate had been broken down by Monk's soldiers during the civil war, and had never been replaced, therefore presented no obstacle to Bothwell and his party. The avenue, very steep and narrow, and causewayed with large round stones, ascended the side of the precipitous bank in an oblique and zigzag course, now showing now hiding a view of the tower and its exterior bulwarks, which seemed to

rise almost perpendicularly above their heads. The fragments of Gothic defences which it exhibited were upon such a scale of strength as induced Bothwell to exclaim, ' It's well this place is in honest and loyal hands. Egad, if the enemy had it, a dozen of old whigamore wives with their distaffs might keep it against a troop of dragoons, at least if they had half the spunk of the old girl we left at Milnwood. Upon my life,' he continued, as they came in front of the large double tower and its surrounding defences and flankers, ' it is a superb place, founded, says the worn inscription over the gate—unless the remnant of my Latin has given me the slip—by sir Ralph de Bellenden in 1350—a respectable antiquity. I must greet the old lady with due honour, though it should put me to the labour of recalling some of the compliments that I used to dabble in when I was wont to keep that sort of company.'

As he thus communed with himself, the butler, who had reconnoitered the soldiers from an arrow-slit in the wall, announced to his lady, that a commanded party of dragoons waited at the gate with a prisoner under their charge.

' I am certain,' said Gudyill, ' and positive, that the sixth man is a prisoner, for his horse is led, and the two dragoons that are before have their carabines out of their budgets and rested upon their thighs. It was aye the way we guarded prisoners in the days of the great marquis.'

' King's soldiers?' said the lady; ' probably in want of refreshment. Go, Gudyill, make them welcome, and let them be accommodated with what provision and forage the tower can afford.—And

stay, tell my gentlewoman to bring my black scarf
and manteau. I will go down myself to receive
them; one cannot show them too much respect in
times when they are doing so much for royal authority. And d'ye hear, Gudyill, let Jenny Dennison slip on her pearlings to walk before my niece
and me, and the three women to walk behind; and
bid my niece attend me instantly.'

Fully accoutred, and attended according to her
directions, lady Margaret now sailed out into the
court-yard of her tower with great courtesy and
dignity. Serjeant Bothwell saluted the grave and
reverend lady of the manor with an assurance which
had something of the light and careless address of
the dissipated men of fashion in Charles the Second's time, and did not at all savour of the awk-
ward or rude manners of a non-commissioned officer of dragoons. His language, as well as his manners, seemed also to be refined for the time and occasion; though the truth was, that, in the fluctua-
tions of an adventurous and profligate life, Bothwell had sometimes kept company much better suited to his ancestry than to his present situation of
life. To the lady's request to know whether she
could be of service to them, he answered, with a
suitable bow, ' That as they had to march some
miles farther that night, they would be much accommodated by permission to rest their horses for
an hour before continuing their journey.'

' With the greatest pleasure,' answered lady
Margaret, ' and I trust that my people will see that
neither horse nor men want suitable refreshment.'

' We are well aware, madam,' continued Bothwell, ' that such has always been the reception, with-

in the walls of Tillietudlem, of those who served the king.'

'We have studied to discharge our duty faithfully and loyally on all occasions, sir,' answered lady Margaret, pleased with the compliment, 'both to our monarchs and to their followers, particularly to their faithful soldiers. It is not long ago, and it probably has not escaped the recollection of his sacred majesty, now on the throne, since he himself honoured my poor house with his presence, and breakfasted in a room in this castle, Mr. Serjeant, which my waiting-gentlewoman shall show you; we still call it the king's room.'

Bothwell had by this time dismounted his party, and committed the horses to the charge of one file, and the prisoner to that of another, so that he himself was at liberty to continue the conversation which the lady had so condescendingly opened.

'Since the king, my master, had the honour to experience your hospitality, I cannot wonder that it is extended to those that serve him, and whose principal merit is doing it with fidelity. And yet I have a nearer relation to his majesty than this coarse red coat would seem to indicate.'

'Indeed, sir? Probably,' said lady Margaret, 'you have belonged to his household?'

'Not exactly, madam, to his household, but rather to his *house*, a connection through which I may claim kindred with most of the best families in Scotland, not, I believe, exclusive of that of Tillietudlem.'

'Sir?' said the old lady, drawing herself up with dignity at hearing what she conceived an impertinent jest, 'I do not understand you.'

'It's but a foolish subject for one in my situation
to talk of, madam,' answered the trooper, 'but you
must have heard of the history and misfortunes of
my grandfather, Francis Stuart, to whom James I.,
his cousin-german, gave the title of Bothwell, as
my comrades give me the nick-name. It was not
in the long run more advantageous to him than it
is to me.'

'Indeed?' said lady Margaret, with much sympathy and surprise; 'I have indeed always under-
stood that the grandson of the last earl was in ne-
cessitous circumstances, but I should never have
expected to see him so low in the service. With
such connections, what ill fortune could have reduced you'——

'Nothing much out of the ordinary course, I believe, madam,' said Bothwell, interrupting and an-
ticipating the question. 'I have had my moments
of good luck like my neighbours—have drank my
bottle with Rochester, thrown a merry main with
Buckingham, and fought at Tangiers side by side
with Sheffield. But my luck never lasted; I could
not make useful friends out of my jolly companions
—Perhaps I was not sufficiently aware,' he continued with some bitterness, 'how much the descendant of the Scotish Stuarts was honoured by being
admitted into the convivialities of Wilmot and Vil-
liers.'

'But your Scotish friends, Mr. Stuart, your re-
lations here, so numerous and so powerful?'

'Why, ay, my lady, I believe some of them might
have made me their gamekeeper, for I am a tolerable shot—some of them would have entertained me
as their bravo, for I can use my sword well—and

here and there was one, who, when better company was not to be had, would have made me his companion, since I can drink my three bottles of wine. —But I don't know how it is—between service and service among my kinsmen, I prefer that of my cousin Charles as the most creditable of them all, although the pay is but poor and the livery far from splendid.'

' It is a shame, it is a burning scandal,' said lady Margaret. ' Why do you not apply to his most sacred majesty? he cannot but be surprised to hear that a scion of his august family'——

' I beg your pardon, madam,' interrupted the serjeant, ' I am but a blunt soldier, and I trust you will excuse me when I say, his most sacred majesty is more busy in grafting scions of his own than with nourishing those which were planted by his grandfather's grandfather.'

' Well, Mr. Stuart,' said lady Margaret, ' one thing you must promise me—remain at Tillietudlem to-night; to-morrow I expect your commanding-officer, the gallant Claverhouse, to whom king and country are so much obliged for his exertions against those who would turn the world upside down. I will speak to him on the subject of your speedy promotion, and I am certain he feels too much, both what is due to the blood which is in your veins, and to the request of a lady so highly distinguished as myself by his most sacred majesty, not to make better provision for you than you have yet received.'

' I am much obliged to your ladyship, and I certainly will remain here with my prisoner, since you request it, especially as it will be the earliest way of presenting him to colonel Grahame, and obtaining his ultimate orders about the young spark.'

'Who is your prisoner, pray you?' said lady Margaret.

'A young fellow of rather the better class in this neighbourhood, who has been so incautious as to give countenance to one of the murderers of the primate, and to facilitate the dog's escape.'

'O, fie upon him!' said lady Margaret, 'I am but too apt to forgive the injuries I have received at the hands of these rogues, though some of them, Mr. Stuart, are of a kind not like to be forgotten; but those who would abet the perpetrators of so cruel and deliberate a homicide on a single man, an old man, and a man of the archbishop's sacred profession—O fie upon him! If you wish to make him secure, with little trouble to your people, I will cause Harrison, or Gudyill, look for the key of our pit, or principal dungeon. It has not been opened since the week after the victory of Kilsythe, when my poor sir Arthur Bellenden put twenty whigs into it; but it is not more than two stories beneath ground, so it cannot be unwholesome, especially as I believe there is somewhere an opening to the outer air.'

'I beg your pardon, madam,' answered the serjeant; 'I dare say the dungeon is a most admirable one, but I have promised to be civil to the lad, and I wil take care he is watched so as to render escape impossible. I'll set those to look after him shall keep him as fast as if his legs were in the boots, or his fingers in the thumbkins.'

'Well, Mr. Stuart,' rejoined the lady, 'you best know your own duty. I heartily wish you good

evening, and commit you to the care of my steward, Harrison. I would ask you to keep us company, but a—a—a—'

'O madam, it requires no apology; I am sensible the coarse red coat of king Charles II does
and ought to annihilate the privileges of the red
blood of king James V.'

'Not with me, I do assure you, Mr. Stuart; you
do me injustice if you think so. I will speak to
your officer to-morrow; you shall soon find yourself
in a rank where there shall need no anomalies to be
reconciled.'

'I believe, madam,' said Bothwell, 'your goodness will find itself deceived; but I am obliged to
you for your intention, and, at all events, I will
have a merry night with Mr. Harrison.'

Lady Margaret took a ceremonious leave, with
all the respect which she owed to royal blood, even
when flowing in the veins of a serjeant of the life-
guards, again assuring Mr. Stuart, that whatever
was in the Tower of Tillietudlem was heartily at
his service and that of his attendants.

Serjeant Bothwell did not fail to take the lady at
her word, and readily forgot the height from which
his family had descended, in a joyous carousal, during which Mr. Harrison exerted himself to produce
the best wine in the cellar, and to excite his guest
to be merry by that seducing example, which, in
matters of conviviality, goes farther than precept.
Old Gudyill associated himself with a party so
much to his taste, pretty much as Davy in the second part of Henry the fourth mingles in the revels
of his master, justice Shallow. He ran down to the
cellar at the risk of breaking his neck, to ransack

some private catacomb, known, as he boasted, only to himself, and which never either had, or should, during his superintendance, render forth a bottle of its contents to any one but a real king's friend.

'When the duke dined here,' said the butler, seating himself at a distance from the table, being somewhat overawed by Bothwell's genealogy, but yet hitching his seat half a yard nearer at every clause of his speech, ' my leddy was importunate to have a bottle of that Burgundy,' (here he advanced his seat a little)—' but I dinna ken how it was, Mr. Stuart, I misdoubted him. I jaloused him, sir, no to be the friend to government he pretends; the family are not to lippen to. That auld Duke James lost his heart before he lost his head; and the Worcester man was but wersh parritch, neither gude to fry, boil, nor sup cauld.' (With this witty observation he completed his first parallel, and commenced a zigzag after the manner of an experienced engineer, in order to continue his approaches to the table.) 'Sae, sir, the faster my leddy cried ' Burgundy to his Grace—the auld Burgundy—the choice Burgundy—the Burgundy that cam ower in the thirty-nine'—the mair did I say to mysel, de'il a drap gangs down his hause unless I was mair sensible o' his principles; sack and claret may serve him. Na, na, gentlemen, as lang as I hae the trust o' butler in this house o' Tillietudlem, I'll tak it upon me to see that nae disloyal or doubtfu' person is the better o' our binns. But when I can find a true friend to the king and his cause, and a moderate episcopacy; when I find a man, as I say, that will stand by church and crown as I did mysel in my master's life, and all through Montrose's time,

I think there is naething in the cellar ower gude to be spared on him.'

By this time he had completed a lodgment in the body of the place, or, in other words, advanced his seat close to the table.

'And now, Mr. Francis Stuart of Bothwell, I have the honour to drink your gude health, and a commission t'ye, and much luck may ye have in raking this country clear o' whigs and round-heads, fanatics and covenanters.'

Bothwell, who, it may well be believed, had long ceased to be very scrupulous in point of society, which he regulated more by his convenience and station in life than his ancestry, readily answered the butler's pledge, acknowledging at the same time, the excellence of the wine; and Mr. Gudyill, thus adopted a regular member of the company, continued to furnish them with the means of mirth until an early hour in the next morning.

CHAPTER X.

Did I but purpose to embark with thee
On the smooth surface of a summer sea,
And would forsake the skiff and make the shore
When the winds whistle and the tempests roar?

Prior.

WHILE Lady Margaret held, with the high-descended serjeant of dragoons, the conference which we have detailed in the preceding pages, her granddaughter, partaking in a less degree her ladyship's

enthusiasm for all who were descended of the blood-
royal, did not honour Serjeant Bothwell with more
attention than a single glance, which showed her a
tall powerful person, and a set of hardy weather-
beaten features, to which pride and dissipation had
given an air where discontent mingled with the
reckless gayety of desperation. The other soldiers
offered still less to detach her consideration; but
from the prisoner, muffled and disguised as he was,
she found it impossible to withdraw her eyes. Yet
she blamed herself for indulging a curiosity which
seemed obviously to give pain to him who was its
object.

' I wish,' she said to Jenny Dennison, who was
the immediate attendant on her person, ' I wish we
knew who that poor fellow is.'

' I was just thinking sae mysel, Miss Edith; but
it canna be Cuddie Headrigg, because he's taller
and no sae stout.'

' Yet,' continued Miss Bellenden, ' it may be some
poor neighbour for whom we might have cause to
interest ourselves.'

' I can sune learn wha he is, if the sodgers were
anes settled and at leisure, for I ken ane o' them
very weel—the best-looking and the youngest o'
them.'

' I think you know all the idle young fellows
about the country,' answered her mistress.

' Na, Miss Edith, I am no sae free o' my acquaintance as that. To be sure, folk canna help
kenning the folk by head-mark that they see aye
glowring and looking at them at kirk and market;
but I ken few lads to speak to unless it be them o'
the family, and the three Steinsons, and Tam Rand,

and the young miller, and the five Howisons in Nethersheils, and lang Tam Gilry, and'——

'Pray cut short a list of exceptions which threatens to be a long one, and tell me how you come to know this young soldier,' said Miss Bellenden.

'Lord, Miss Edith, it's Tam Halliday, Trooper Tam, as they ca' him, that was wounded by the hill-folk at the conventicle at Outer-side-Muir, and lay here while he was under cure. I can ask him ony thing, and Tam will not refuse to answer me, I'll be caution for him.'

'Try, then, said Miss Edith, ' if you can find an opportunity to ask him the name of his prisoner, and come to my room and tell me what he says.'

Jenny Dennison proceeded on her errand, but soon returned with such a face of surprise and dismay as evinced a deep interest in the fate of the prisoner.

'What is the matter?' said Edith, anxiously; ' does it prove to be Cuddie, after all, poor fellow?'

'Cuddie, Miss Edith? Na! na! it's nae Cuddie,' blubbered out the faithful fille-de-chambre, sensible of the pain which her news were about to inflict on her young mistress. ' O dear, Miss Edith, it's young Milnwood himsel!'

'Young Milnwood?' exclaimed Edith, aghast in her turn; ' it is impossible—totally impossible!— His uncle attends the clergyman indulged by law, and has no connexion whatever with the refractory people; and he himself has never interfered in this unhappy dissention; he must be totally innocent unless he has been standing up for some invaded right.'

'O, my dear Miss Edith,' said her attendant, ' these are not days to ask what's right or what' wrang; if he were as innocent as the new-born infant, they would find some way of making him guilty, if they liked; but Tam Halliday says it will touch his life, for he has been resetting ane o' the Fife gentlemen that killed that auld carle of an Archbishop.'

'His life!' exclaimed Edith, starting hastily up and speaking with a hurried and tremulous accent,— ' they cannot—they shall not—I will speak with him —they shall not hurt him!'

'O, my dear young leddy, think on your grandmother; think on the danger and the difficulty,' added Jenny; 'for he's kept under close confinement till Claverhouse comes up in the morning, and if he does na gi'e him full satisfaction, Tam Halliday says there will be brief wark wi' him—Kneel down—mak ready—present—fire—just as they did wi' auld deaf John Macbriar, that never heard a question they pat till him, and lost his life for lack o' hearing.'

'Jenny,' said the young lady, 'if he should die, I will die with him; there is no time to talk of danger or difficulty—I will put on a plaid, and slip down with you to the place where they have kept him—I will throw myself at the feet of the centinel, and entreat him, as he has a soul to be saved'——

'Eh guide us!' interrupted the maid, 'our young leddy at the feet o' Trooper Tam, and speaking to him about his soul, when the puir chield hardly kens whether he has ane or no, unless that he whiles swears by it—that will never do; but what maun be maun be, and I'll never desert a true-love cause—An' sae, if ye maun see young Milnwood, though I ken nae gude it will do, but to make baith your hearts the sairer, I'll e'en tak the risk o't and try to

manage Tam Halliday; but ye maun let me hae my
ain gate and no speak ae word—he's keeping guard
o'er Milnwood in the easter round of the tower.'

'Go, go, fetch me a plaid,' said Edith, 'Let me
but see him, and I will find some remedy for his
danger—Haste ye, Jenny, as ever you hope to have
good at my hands.'

Jenny hastened, and soon returned with a plaid,
in which Edith muffled herself so as completely to
screen her face, and in part to disguise her person.
This was a mode of arranging the plaid very common among the ladies of that century, and the earlier part of the succeeding one; so much so indeed,
that the venerable sages of the Kirk, conceiving that
the mode gave tempting facilities for intrigue, directed more than one act of Assembly against this
use of the mantle. But fashion, as usual, proved too
strong for authority, and while plaids continued to
be worn, women of all ranks occasionally employed
them as a sort of muffler or veil. Her face and figure
thus concealed, Edith, holding by her attendant's
arm, hastened with trembling steps to the place of
Morton's confinement.

This was a small study, or closet, in one of the
turrets, opening upon a gallery in which the centinel
was pacing to and fro; for Serjeant Bothwell, scrupulous in observing his word, and perhaps touched
with some compassion for the prisoner's youth and
genteel demeanour, had waived the indignity of
putting his guard into the same apartment with him.
Halliday, therefore, with his carabine on his arm,
walked up and down the gallery, occasionally solac-
ing himself with a draught of ale, a huge flagon of
which stood upon a table at one end of the apart-

ment, and at other times humming the lively Scotish air,

> ' Between Saint Johnstone and Bonny Dundee,
> I'll gar ye be fain to follow me,'——

Jenny Dennison cautioned her mistress once more
to let her take her own way.

' I can manage the trooper weel eneugh,' she said,
' for as rough as he is—I ken their nature weel; but
ye maunna say a single word.'

She accordingly opened the door of the gallery
just as the centinel had turned his back from it, and,
taking up the tune which he hummed, she sung in
a coquettish tone of rustic raillery,

> ' If I were to follow a poor sodger lad,
> My friends wad be angry, my minnie be mad;
> A laird, or a lord, they were fitter for me,
> Sae I'll never be fain to follow thee.'——

' A fair challenge, by Jove,' cried the centinel,
turning round, ' and from two at once, but it's not
easy to bang the soldier with his bandeliers;' then
taking up the song where the damsel had stopt,

> ' To follow me ye weel may be glad,
> A share of my supper, a share of my bed,
> To the sound of the drum to range fearless and free,
> I'll gar ye be fain to follow me.'——

' Come, my pretty nurse, and kiss me for my
song.'

' I should not have thought of that, Mr. Halliday,' answered Jenny, with a look and tone ex-

pressing just the necessary degree of contempt at
the proposal, ' and, I'se assure ye, ye'll hae but little
o' my company unless ye shew gentler havings—
It wasna to hear that sort o' nonsense that brought
me here wi' my friend, and ye should think shame
o' yoursel, 'at should ye.'

' Umph! and what sort of nonsense did bring you
here then, Mrs. Dennison?'

' My kinswoman has some particular business
with your prisoner, young Mr. Harry Morton, and
I am come wi' her to speak till him.'

' The devil you are,' answered the centinel; ' and
pray, Mrs. Dennison, how do your kinswoman and
you propose to get in? You are rather too plump to
whisk through a key-hole, and opening the door is
a thing not to be spoke of.'

' It's no a thing to be spoken o', but a thing to be
dune,' replied the persevering damsel.

' We'll see about that, my bonny Jenny;' and the
soldier resumed his march, humming, as he walked
to and fro along the gallery.

> ' Keek into the draw-well,
> Janet, Janet,
> Then ye'll see your bonny sell,
> My joe Janet.'

' So ye're no thinking to let us in, Mr. Halliday?
Weel, weel—gude e'en to you—ye hae seen the last
o' me, and o' this bonny-dye too,' said Jenny, holding
between her finger and thumb a silver dollar.

' Give him gold, give him gold,' whispered the
agitated young lady.

' Silver's e'en ower gude for the like o' him, that
disna care for the blink o' a bonny lassie's e'e—and

what's waur, he wad think there was something
mair in't than a kinswoman o' mine.   My sarty!
siller's no sae plenty wi' us, let alane gowd.'   Having addressed this advice aside to her mistress, she
raised her voice, and said, ' My cousin winna stay
ony langer, Mr. Halliday; sae, if ye please, gude
e'en t'ye.'

' Halt a bit, halt a bit,' said the trooper; ' rein up
and parley, Jenny.   If I let your kinswoman in to
speak to my prisoner, you must stay here and keep
me company till she come out again, and then we'll
all be well pleased you know.'

' The fiend be in my feet then,' said Jenny; ' d'ye
think my kinswoman and me are gaun to lose our
gude name wi' cracking clavers wi' the like o' you
or your prisoner either, without somebody by to see
fair play? Hegh, hegh, sirs, to see sic a difference
between folk's promises and performance! Ye were
aye willing to slight puir Cuddie; but an' I had
asked him to oblige me in a thing, though it had
been to cost his hanging, he wadna hae stude twice
about it.'

' D——n Cuddie,' retorted the dragoon, ' he'll be
hanged in good earnest, I hope.   I saw him to-day
at Milnwood with his old puritanical b—— of a
mother, and if I had thought I was to have had
him cast in my dish, I would have brought him
up at my horse's tail—we had law enough to bear
us out.'

' Very weel, very weel—See if Cuddie winna
hae a lang shot at you ane o' thae days, if ye gaur
him tak the muir wi' sae mony honest folk. He can
hit a mark brawly; he was third at the popinjay;
and he's as true of his promise as of e'e and hand,

though he disna mak sic a phrase about it as some acquaintance o' yours—But it's a' ane to me—Come, cousin, we'll awa'.'

'Stay, Jenny; d—n me, if I hang fire more than another when I have said a thing,' said the soldier in a hesitating tone. 'Where is the serjeant?'

'Drinking and driving ower,' quoth Jenny, 'wi' the steward and John Gudyill.'

'So, so—he's safe enough—and where are my comrades?' said the centinel.

'Birling the brown bowl wi' the fowler and the falconer, and some o' the serving folk.'

'Have they plenty of ale?'

'Sax gallons, as gude as e'er was masked,' said the maid.

'Well, then, my pretty Jenny,' said the relenting centinel, 'they are fast till the hour of relieving guard, and perhaps something later; and so, if you will promise to come alone the next time'——

'Maybe I will, and maybe I winna,' said Jenny; 'but if ye get the dollar, ye'll like that just as weel.'

'I'll be d—n'd if I do,' said Halliday, taking the money however; 'but it's always something for my risk; for, if Claverhouse hears what I have done, he will build me a horse as high as the tower of Tillietudlem. But every one in the regiment takes what they can come by; I am sure Bothwell and his blood-royal shows us a good example. And if I were trusting to you, you little jilting devil, I should lose both pains and powder; whereas this fellow,' looking at the piece, 'will be good as far as he goes. So, come, there is the door open for you; do not stay groaning and praying with the young whig now, but be ready, when I call at the door, to start, as if they were sounding "Horse and away."'

So speaking, Halliday unlocked the door of the closet, admitted Jenny and her pretended kinswoman, locked it behind them, and hastily reassumed the indifferent measured step and time-killing whistle of a centinel upon his regular duty.

The door, which slowly opened, discovered Morton with both arms reclined upon a table, and his head resting upon them in a posture of deep dejection. He raised his face as the door opened, and, perceiving the female figures which it admitted, started up in great surprise. Edith, as if modesty had quelled the courage which despair had bestowed, stood about a yard from the door without having either the power to speak or to advance. All the plans of aid, relief, or comfort, which she had proposed to lay before her lover, seemed at once to have vanished from her recollection, and left only a painful chaos of ideas, with which was mingled a fear that she had degraded herself in the eyes of her lover by a step which might appear precipitate and unfeminine. She hung motionless and almost powerless upon the arm of her attendant, who in vain endeavoured to reassure and inspire her with courage, by whispering, ' We are in now, madam, and we maun mak the best o' our time; for, doubtless, the corporal or the serjeant will gang the rounds, and it wad be a pity to hae the poor lad Halliday punished for his civility.'

Morton, in the mean time, was timidly advancing, suspecting the truth; for what other female in the house, excepting Edith herself, was likely to take an interest in his misfortunes? and yet afraid, owing to the doubtful twilight and the muffled dress, of making some mistake which might be prejudicial to the object of his affections. Jenny, whose ready wit and forward manners well qualified her for such an office, hastened to break the ice.

'Mr. Morton, miss Edith's very sorry for your present situation, and'——

It was needless to say more; he was at her side almost at her feet, pressing her unresisting hands, and loading her with a profusion of thanks and gratitude which would be hardly intelligible from the mere broken words, unless we could describe the tone, the gesture, the impassioned and hurried indications of deep and tumultuous feeling with which they were accompanied.

For two or three minutes, Edith stood as motionless as the statue of a saint which receives the adoration of a worshipper; and when she recovered herself sufficiently to withdraw her hands from Henry's grasp, she could at first only faintly articulate, 'I have taken a strange step, Mr. Morton—a step,' she continued with more coherence, as her ideas arranged themselves in consequence of a strong effort, 'that perhaps may expose me to censure in your eyes—But I have long permitted you to use the language of friendship—perhaps I might say more—too long to leave you when the world seems to have left you. How, or why, is this imprisonment? what can be done? can my uncle, who thinks so highly of you—can your own kinsman, Milnwood, be of no use? are there no means? and what is likely to be the event?'

'Be what it will,' answered Henry, contriving to make himself master of the hand that had escaped from him, but which was now again abandoned to his clasp, ' be what it will, it is to me from this moment the most welcome incident of a weary life. To you, dearest Edith—forgive me, I should have said miss Bellenden, but misfortune claims strange privileges—to you I have owed the few happy moments which have gilded a gloomy existence; and if I am now to lay it down, the recollection of this honour will be my happiness in the last hour of suffering.'

' But is it even thus, Mr. Morton? Have you, who used to mix so little in these unhappy feuds, become so suddenly and deeply implicated, that nothing short of'—

She paused, unable to bring out the word which should have come next.

' Nothing short of my life you would say?' replied Morton, in a calm, but melancholy tone; ' I believe that will be entirely in the bosoms of my judges. My guards spoke of a possibility of exchanging the penalty for entry into foreign service. I thought I could have embraced the alternative; and yet, miss Bellenden, since I have seen you once more, I feel that exile would be more galling than death.'

' And is it then true,' said Edith, ' that you have been so desperately rash as to entertain communication with any of those cruel wretches who assassinated the primate?'

' I knew not even that such a crime had been committed,' replied Morton, ' when I gave unhappily a night's lodging and concealment to one of those rash men, the ancient friend and comrade of my father. But my ignorance will avail me little;

for who, miss Bellenden, save you, will believe it?
And, what is worse, I am at least uncertain whether, even if I had known the crime, I could have
brought my mind, under all the circumstances, to
refuse a temporary refuge to the fugitive.'

'And by whom,' said Edith, anxiously, 'or under what authority, will the investigation of your
conduct take place?'

'Under that of colonel Grahame of Claverhouse,
I am given to understand,' said Morton; 'one of
the military commission, to whom it has pleased
our king, our privy council, and our parliament
that used to be more tenacious of our liberties, to
commit the sole charge of our goods and of our
lives.'

'To Claverhouse?' said Edith, faintly; 'merci-
ful Heaven, you are lost ere you are tried! He
wrote to my grand-mother that he was to be here
to-morrow morning, on his road to the head of the
country, where some desperate men are said to have
assembled for the purpose of making a stand, animated by the presence of two or three of the actors
in the primate's murder. His expressions made me
shudder, even when I could not guess that—that—
a friend'——

'Do not be too much alarmed on my account, my
dearest Edith,' said Henry, as he supported her in
his arms; 'Claverhouse, though stern and relentless, is, by all accounts, brave, fair, and honourable.
I am a soldier's son, and will plead my cause like a
soldier. He will perhaps listen more favourably to
a blunt and unvarnished defence than a tricking and
time-serving judge might do. And, indeed, in a
time when justice is, in all its branches, so com-

pletely corrupted, I would rather lose my life by open military violence, than be conjured out of it by the hocus-pocus of some arbitrary lawyer, who lends the knowledge he has of the statutes made for our protection, to wrest them to our destruction.'

' You are lost—you are lost, if you are to plead your cause with Claverhouse!' sighed Edith; ' root and branch-work was the mildest of his expressions. The unhappy primate was his intimate friend and early patron. ' " No excuse, no subterfuge," said his letter, " shall save either those connected with the deed, or such as have given them countenance and shelter, from the ample and bitter penalty of the law, until I shall have taken as many lives in vengeance of this atrocious murder, as the old man had gray hairs upon his venerable head." There is neither ruth nor favour to be found with him.'

Jenny Dennison, who had hitherto remained silent, now ventured, in the extremity of distress, which the lovers felt, but for which they were unable to devise a remedy, to offer her own advice.

' Wi' your leddyship's pardon, miss Edith, and young Mr. Milnwood's, we maunna waste time. Let Milnwood take my plaid and gown; I'll slip them aff in the dark corner, if he'll promise no to look about, and he may walk past Tam Halliday, who is half blind with his ale, and I can tell him a canny way to get out o' the Tower, and your leddyship will gang quietly to your ain room, and I'll row mysel in his gray cloak, and pit on his hat, and play the prisoner till the coast's clear, and then I'll cry in Tam Halliday and gar him let me out.'

' Let you out?' said Morton; ' they'll make your life answer it.'

'Ne'er a bit,' replied Jenny; 'Tam daurna tell he let ony body in, for his ain sake; and I'll gar him find some other gate to account for the escape.'

'Will you, by G——?' said the centinel, suddenly opening the door of the apartment; 'if I am half blind, I am not deaf, and you should not plan an escape quite so loud, if you expect to go through with it. Come, come, Mrs. Janet—march, troop—quick time—trot, d—n me!—And you, madam kinswoman,—I won't ask your real name, though you were going to play me so rascally a trick,—but I must make a clear garrison; so beat a retreat, unless you would have me turn out the guard.'

'I hope,' said Morton, very anxiously, 'you will not mention this circumstance, my good friend, and trust to my honour to acknowledge your civility in keeping the secret. If you overheard our conversation, you must have observed that we did not accept of, or enter into, the hasty proposal made by this good-natured girl.'

'Oh, devilish good-natured, to be sure,' said Halliday. 'As for the rest, I guess how it is, and I scorn to bear malice, or tell tales, as much as another; but no thanks to that little jilting devil, Jenny Dennison, who deserves a tight skelping for trying to lead an honest lad into a scrape, just because he was so silly as to like her good-for-little chit face.'

Jenny had no better means of justification than the last apology to which her sex trust, and usually not in vain; she pressed her handkerchief to her face, sobbed with great vehemence, and either wept, or managed, as Halliday might have said, to go through the motions wonderfully well.

'And now,' continued the soldier, somewhat mollified, 'if you have any thing to say, say it in two minutes, and let me see your backs turned; for if Bothwell take it into his drunken head to make the rounds half an hour too soon, it will be a black business to us all.'

'Farewell, Edith,' whispered Morton, assuming a firmness he was far from possessing; 'do not remain here—leave me to my fate—it cannot be beyond endurance since you are interested in it.— Good night, good night!—Do not remain here till you are discovered.'——

Thus saying, he resigned her to her attendant, by whom she was partly led and partly supported out of the apartment.

'Every one has his taste, to be sure,' said Halliday; 'but d—n me if I would have vexed so sweet a girl as that is, for all the whigs that ever swore the Covenant.'

When Edith had regained her apartment, she gave way to a burst of grief which alarmed Jenny Dennison, who hastened to administer such scraps of consolation as occurred to her.

'Dinna vex yoursel sae muckle, miss Edith,' said that faithful attendant; 'wha kens what may happen to help young Milnwood? He's a brave lad, and a bonny, and a gentleman of a good fortune, and they winna string the like o' him up as they do the puir whig bodies that they catch in the muirs, like straps o' onions; maybe his uncle will bring him aff, or maybe your ain granduncle will speak a gude word for him—he's weel acquent wi' a' the red-coat gentlemen.'

' You are right, Jenny! you are right,' said Edith, recovering herself from the stupor into which she had sunk; ' this is no time for despair, but for exertion. You must find some one to ride this very night to my uncle's with a letter.'

' To Charnwood, madam? It's unco late, and it's sax miles an' a bittock doun the water; I doubt if we can find man and horse the night, mair especially as they hae mounted a centinel before the gate. Puir Cuddie! he's gane, puir fallow, that wad hae dune aught in the warld I bade him, and ne'er asked a reason—an' I've had nae time to draw up wi' the new pleugh-lad yet; forby that, they say he's gaun to be married to Meg Murdieson, ill-fa'ard cuttie as she is.'

' You *must* find some one to go, Jenny; life and death depend upon it.'

' I wad gang mysel, my leddy, for I could creep out at the window o' the pantry, and speel down by the auld yew-tree weel eneugh—I hae played that trick ere now. But the road's unca wild, and sae mony red-coats about, forby the whigs, that are no muckle better (the young lads o' them,) if they meet a fraim body their lane in the muirs. I wadna stand for the walk—I can walk ten miles by moonlight weel eneugh.'

' Is there no one you can think of, that, for money or favour, would serve me so far?' said Edith, in great anxiety.

' I dinna ken,' said Jenny, after a moment's consideration, ' unless it be Guse Gibbie; and he'll maybe no ken the way, though it's no sae difficult to hit, if he keep the horse-road, and mind the turn at the Cappercleuch, and dinna drown himsel in

Whomlekirn-pule, or fa' ower the scaur at the Dei'l's Loaning, or miss ony o' the kittle staps at the Pass o' Walkwary, or be carried to the hills by the whigs, or be ta'en to the tolbooth by the red-coats.'

'All ventures must be run,' said Edith, cutting short the list of chances against Goose Gibbie's safe arrival at the end of his pilgrimage; 'all risks must be run, unless you can find a better messen-ger.—Go, bid the boy get ready, and get him out of the tower as secretly as you can. If he meets any one, let him say he is carrying a letter to major Bellenden of Charnwood, but without mentioning any names.'

'I understand, madam,' said Jenny Dennison; 'I warrant the callant will do weel aneugh, and Tib the hen-wife will tak care o' the geese for a word o' my mouth; and I'll tell Gibbie your leddyship will mak his peace wi' lady Margaret, and will gi'e him a dollar.'

'Two, if he does his errand well,' said Edith.

Jenny departed to rouse Goose Gibbie out of his slumbers, to which he was usually consigned at sun-down, or shortly after, he keeping the hours of the birds under his charge. During her absence, Edith took her writing materials, and prepared against her return the following letter, superscribed, For the hands of major Bellenden of Charnwood, my much honoured uncle, These:

'My dear Uncle—This will serve to inform you I am desirous to know how your gout is, as we did not see you at the wappin-schaw, which made both my grandmother and myself very uneasy. And if will permit you to travel, we will be happy to see you at our poor house to-morrow at the hour of breakfast, as colonel Grahame of Claverhouse is to pass this way on his march, and we would willingly have your assistance to receive and entertain a military man of such distinction, who, probably, will not be much delighted with the company of women. Also, my dear uncle, I pray you to let Mrs. Carfoot, your house-keeper, send me my double-trimmed paduasoy with the hanging sleeves, which she will find in the third drawer of the walnut press in the green room, which you are so kind as to call mine. Also, my dear uncle, I pray you to send me the second volume of the Grand Cyrus, as I have only read as far as the imprisonment of Philidaspes upon the seven hundredth and thirty-third page; but, above all, I entreat you to come to us to-morrow before eight of the clock, which, as your pacing nag is so good, you may well do without rising before your usual hour. So, praying to God to preserve your health, I rest your dutiful and loving niece,

'EDITH BELLENDEN.

' *Postscriptum.* A party of soldiers have last night brought your friend, young Mr. Henry Morton of Milnwood, hither as a prisoner. I conclude you will be sorry for the young gentleman, and, therefore, let you know this, in case you may think of speaking to colonel Grahame in his behalf. I have not mentioned his name to my grandmother, knowing her prejudice against the family.'

This epistle being duly sealed and delivered to Jenny, that faithful confidante hastened to put the same in the charge of Goose Gibbie, whom she found in readiness to start from the castle. She then gave him various instructions touching the road which she apprehended he was likely to mistake, not having travelled it above five or six times, and possessing only the same slender proportion of memory as of judgment. Lastly, she smuggled him out of the garrison through the pantry window into the branchy yew-tree which grew close beside it, and had the satisfaction to see him reach the bottom in safety, and take the right turn at the commencement of his journey. She then returned to persuade her young mistress to go to bed, and to lull her to rest, if possible, with assurances of Gibbie's success in his embassy, only qualified by a passing regret that the trusty Cuddie, with whom the commission might have been more safely reposed, was no longer within reach of serving her.

More fortunate as a messenger than as a cavalier, it was Gibbie's good hap, rather than his good management, which, after he had gone astray not oftener than nine times, and given his garments a taste of the variation of each bog, brook, and slough, between Tillietudlem and Charnwood, placed him about day-break before the gate of major Bellenden's mansion, having completed a walk of ten miles (for the bittock, as usual, amounted to four) in little more than the same number of hours.

CHAPTER XI.

At last comes the troop, by the word of command,
Drawn up in our court, where the captain cries, Stand.

Swift.

MAJOR BELLENDEN's ancient valet, Gideon Pike, as he adjusted his master's clothes by his bed-side, preparatory to the worthy veteran's toilet, acquaint-ed him, as an apology for disturbing him an hour earlier than his usual time of rising, that there was an express from Tillietudlem.

'From Tillietudlem?' said the old gentleman, ri-sing hastily in his bed, and sitting bolt upright,—'Open the shutters, Pike—I hope my sister-in-law is well—furl up the bed-curtain.—What have we all here?' (glancing at Edith's note.) 'The gout?—why, she knows I have not had a fit since Candle-mas.—The wappin-schaw? I told her a month since I was not to be there.—Paduasoy and hanging sleeves? why, hang the gipsey herself!—Grand Cy-rus and Philipdastus—Philip Devil—is the wench gone crazy all at once? was it worth while to send an express and wake me at five in the morning for all this trash?—But what says her postscriptum? Mercy on us!' he exclaimed on perusing it,—' Pike, saddle old Kilsythe instantly, and another horse for yourself.'

' I hope nae ill news frae the Tower, sir?' said Pike, astonished at his master's sudden emotion.

' Yes—no—yes—that is, I must meet Claver-house there on some express business; so boot and saddle, Pike, as fast as you can.—O, Lord! what times are these!—the poor lad—my old cronnie's son!—and the silly wench sticks it into her postscriptum, as she calls it, at the tail of all this trumpery about old gowns and new romances!'

In a few minutes the good old officer was fully equipped; and, having mounted upon his arm-gaunt charger as soberly as Mark Antony himself could have done, he paced forth his way to the Tower of Tillietudlem.

On the road he formed the prudent resolution to say nothing to the old lady, (whose dislike to presbyterians of all kinds he knew to be inveterate,) of the quality and rank of the prisoner detained within her walls, but to try his own influence with Claverhouse to obtain Morton's liberation.

'Being so loyal as he is, he must do something for so old a cavalier as I am,' thought the veteran to himself, 'and if he is so good a soldier as the world speaks of, why, he will be glad to serve an old soldier's son. I never knew a real soldier that was not a frank-hearted, honest fellow; and I think the execution of the laws (though its a pity they find it necessary to make them so severe) may be a thousand times better entrusted with them than with peddling lawyers and thick-skulled country gentlemen.'

Such were the ruminations of Major Miles Bellenden, which were terminated by John Gudyill (not more than half drunk) taking hold of his bridle, and assisting him to dismount in the rough paved court of Tillietudlem.

'Why, John,' said the veteran, 'what devil of a discipline is this you have been keeping? You have been reading Geneva print this morning already.'

' I have been reading the Litany,' said John, shaking his head with a look of drunken gravity, and having only caught one word of the Major's address to him; ' life is short, sir; we are flowers of the field, sir,—hiccup—and lilies of the valley.'

' Flowers and lilies? why, man, such carles as thou and I can hardly be called better than old hemlocks, decayed nettles, or withered rag-weed; but I suppose you think that we are still worth watering.'

' I am an old soldier, sir, I thank Heaven'—hiccup.

' An old skinker, you mean, John. But come, never mind, show me the way to your mistress, old lad.'

John Gudyill led the way to the stone hall, where Lady Margaret was fidgetting about, superintending, arranging, and reforming the preparations made for the reception of the celebrated Claverhouse, whom one party honoured and extolled as a hero, and another execrated as a blood-thirsty oppressor.

' Did I not tell you,' said Lady Margaret to her principal female attendant—' did I not tell you, Mysie, that it was my especial pleasure on this occasion to have every thing in the precise order wherein it was upon that famous morning when his most sacred majesty partook of his disjune at Tillietudlem?'

' Doubtless, such were your leddyship's commands, and to the best of my rememberance'—was Mysie answering, when her ladyship broke in with, ' Then wherefore is the venison pasty placed on the left side of the throne, and the stoup of claret upon the right, when ye may right weel remember, My-

sie, that his most sacred majesty with his ain hand
shifted the pasty to the same side with the flagon,
and said they were too good friends to be parted?'

' I mind that weel, madam,' said Mysie; ' and if
I had forgot, I have heard your leddyship often
speak about that grand morning sin' syne; but I
thought every thing was to be placed just as it was
when his majesty, God bless him, came into this
room, looking mair like an angel than a man, if he
hadna been sae black-a-vised.'

' Then ye thought nonsense, Mysie; for in whatever way his most sacred majesty ordered the position of the trenchers and flagons, that, as weel as
his royal pleasure in greater matters, should be a
law to his subjects, and shall ever be to those of the
house of Tillietudlem.'

' Weel, madam,' said Mysie, making the altera-
tion required, ' it's easy mending the error; but if
every thing is just to be as his majesty left it,
there should be an unco hole in the venison pasty.'

At this moment the door opened.

' Who is that, John Gudyill?' exclaimed the old
lady. ' I can speak to no one just now.——Is it you, my
dear brother?' she continued, in some surprise, as
the major entered; ' this is a right early visit.'

' Not more early than welcome I hope?' replied
Major Bellenden, as he saluted the widow of his
deceased brother; ' but I heard by a note which
Edith sent to Charnwood about some of her equipage and books, that you were to have Claver'se
here this morning, so I thought, like an old fire-
lock as I am, that I should like to have a chat with
this rising soldier. I caused Pike saddle Kilsythe,
and here we both are.

' And most kindly welcome you are,' said the old lady; ' it is just what I should have prayed, if I had thought there was time. You see I am busy in preparation. All is to be in the same order as when'——

' The king breakfasted at Tillietudlem,' said the major, who, like all lady Margaret's friends, dreaded the commencement of that narrative, and was desirous to cut it short,—' I remember it well; you know I was waiting on his majesty.'

' You were, brother,' said lady Margaret; ' and perhaps you can help me to remember the order of the entertainment.'

' Nay, good sooth,' said the major, ' the damnable dinner that Noll gave us at Worchester a few days afterwards, drove all your good cheer out of my memory.—But how's this?—you have even the great Turkey-lethern elbow-chair, with the tapestry cushins, placed in state.'

' The throne, brother if you please,' said lady Margaret, gravely.

' Well, the throne be it, then,' continued the major. ' Is that to be Claver'se's post in the attack upon the pasty?'

' No, brother,' said the lady; ' as these cushions have been once honoured by accommodating the person of our most sacred Monarch, they shall never, please Heaven, during my life-time, be pressed by any less dignified weight.'

' You should not put them in the way, then, of an honest old cavalier, who has ridden ten miles before breakfast; for, to confess the truth, they look very inviting. But where is Edith?'

' On the battlements of the warder's turret,' answered the old lady, ' looking out for the approach of our guests.'

' Why, I'll go there too; and so should you, lady Margaret, as soon as you have your line of battle properly formed in the hall here. It's a pretty thing, I can tell you, to see a regiment of horse upon the march.'

Thus speaking, he offered his arm with an air of old-fashioned gallantry, which Lady Margaret accepted with such a curtesy of acknowledgment as ladies were wont to make in Holyrood-house before the year 1642, which, for one while, drove both courtesies and courts out of fashion.

Upon the bartizan of the turret, to which they ascended by many a winding passage and uncouth staircase, they found Edith, not in the attitude of a young lady who watches with fluttering curiosity the approach of a smart regiment of dragoons, but pale, downcast, and evincing, by her countenance, that sleep had not, in the preceding night, been the companion of her pillow. The good old veteran was hurt at her appearance, which, in the hurry of preparation, her grandmother had omitted to notice.

' What is come over you, you silly girl?' he said; ' why, you look like an officer's wife when she opens the News-letter after an action, and expects to find her husband among the killed and wounded. But I know the reason—you will persist in reading these nonsensical romances, day and night, and whimpering for distresses that never existed. Why, how the devil can you believe that Artamines, or what d'ye call him, fought single-handed with a whole battalion? One to three is as great odds as ever fought and won, and I never knew any body that cared to take that except old Corporal Raddlebanes. But these d——d books put all pretty men's actions out of countenance. I dare say you would think very little of Raddlebanes, if he were alongside of Artamines.——I would have the fellows that write such nonsense brought to the picquet for leasing-making.'

Lady Margaret, herself somewhat attached to the perusal of romances, took up the cudgels.

' Monsieur Scuderi,' she said, ' is a soldier, brother, and, as I have heard, a complete one, and so is the Sieur D'Urfe.'

' More shame for them; they should have known better what they were writing about. For my part, I have not read a book these twenty years except my Bible, The Whole Duty of Man, and, of late days, Turner's Pallas Armata, or Treatise on the Ordering of the Pike Exercise, and I don't like *his* discipline much neither. He wants to draw up the cavalry in front of a stand of pikes, instead of being upon the wings. Sure am I, if we had done so at Kilsythe, instead of having our handful of horse on the flanks, the first discharge would have sent them back among our Highlanders.——But I hear the kettle-drums.'

All heads were now bent from the battlements of the turret, which commanded a distant prospect down the vale of the river. The Tower of Tillietudlem stood, or perhaps yet stands, upon the angle of a very precipitous bank, formed by the junction of a considerable brook with the Clyde. There was a narrow bridge of one steep arch, across the brook

near its mouth, over which, and along the foot of
the high and broken bank, winded the public road;
and the fortalice, thus commanding both bridge and
pass, had been, in times of war, a post of considerable importance, the possession of which was necessary to secure the communication of the upper
and wilder districts of the country with those beneath, where the valley expands, and is more capable of cultivation.   The view downwards is of a
grand woodland character; but the leve ground and
gentle slopes near the river form cultivated fields
of an irregular form, interspersed with hedge row
tress and copses, the inclosures seeming as it were
to have been cleared out of the forest which sur-
rounds them, and which occupies, in unbroken
masses, the steeper declivities and more distant
banks. The stream, in colour a clear and sparkling
brown, like the hue of the cairngorum pebbles,
rushes through this romantic region in bold sweeps
and curves, partly visible and partly concealed by
the trees which clothe its banks. With a providence
unknown in other parts of Scotland, the peasants
have, in most places, planted orchards around their
cottages, and the general blossom of the apple-trees
at this season of the year gave all the lower part of
the view the appearance of a flower-garden.

Looking up the river, the character of the scene
was varied considerably for the worse. A hilly,
waste, and uncultivated country approached close
to the banks; the trees were few, and limited to the
neighbourhood of the stream, and the rude moors
swelled at a little distance into shapeless and heavy
hills, which were again surmounted in their turn by
a range of lofty mountains, dimly seen on the hori-

zon. Thus the Tower commanded two prospects, the one richly cultivated and highly adorned, the other exhibiting the monotonous and dreary character of a wild and inhospitable moorland.

The eyes of the spectators on the present occasion were attracted to the downward view, not alone by its superior beauty, but because the distant sounds of military music began to be heard from the public high road which winded up the vale, and announced the approach of the expected body of cavalry. Their glimmering ranks were shortly afterwards seen in the distance, appearing and disappearing as the trees and the windings of the road permitted them to be visible, and distinguished chiefly by the flashes of light which their arms occasionally reflected against the sun. The train was long and imposing, for there were about two hundred and fifty horse upon the march, and the glancing of the swords and waving of their banners, joined to the clang of their trumpets and kettle drums, had at once a lively and awful effect upon the imagination. As they advanced still nearer and nearer, they could distinctly see the files of these chosen troops following each other in long succession, completely equipped and superbly mounted.

'It's a sight that makes me thirty years younger,' said the old cavalier, 'and yet I do not much like the service that these poor fellows are to be engaged in. Although I had my share of the civil war, I cannot say I had ever so much real pleasure in that sort of service as when I was in service on the continent, and we were hacking at fellows with foreign faces and outlandish language. It's a hard

thing to hear a hamely Scotch tongue cry quarter,
and be obliged to cut him down just the same as if
he called out *misericordé*.—So, there they come
through the Netherwood haugh; upon my word,
fine-looking fellows, and capitally mounted—He
that is galloping from the rear of the column must
be Claver'se himsel;—ay, he gets into the front as
they cross the bridge, and now they will be with us
in less than five minutes.'

At the bridge beneath the Tower the cavalry divided, and the greater part, moving up the left bank
of the brook and crossing at a ford a little above,
took the road of the Grange, as it was called, a
large set of farm-offices belonging to the Tower,
where Lady Margaret had ordered preparation to
be made for their reception and suitable entertainment. The officers alone, with their colours and
an escort to guard them, were seen to take the steep
road up to the gate of the Tower, appearing by intervals as they gained the ascent, and again hidden
by projections of the bank and of the huge old trees
with which it is covered. When they emerged from
this narrow path they found themselves in front of
the old Tower, the gates of which were hospitably
open for their reception. Lady Margaret, with
Edith and her brother-in-law, having hastily descended from their post of observation, appeared
to meet and to welcome their guests, with a retinue
of domestics in as good order as the orgies of the
preceding evening permitted. The gallant young
cornet (a relation as well as namesake of Claverhouse, with whom the reader has been already made
acquainted) lowered the standard amid the fanfare
of the trumpets, in homage to the rank of Lady

Margaret and the charms of her grand-daughter, and the old walls echoed to the flourish of the instruments and the stamp and neigh of the chargers.

Claverhouse himself alighted from a black horse, the most beautiful perhaps in Scotland. He had not a single white hair upon his whole body, a circumstance, which, joined to his spirit and fleetness, and to his being so frequently employed in pursuit of the presbyterian recusants, caused an opinion to prevail among them, that the steed had been presented to his rider by the great enemy of mankind in order to assist him in persecuting the fugitive wanderers. When Claverhouse had paid his respects to the ladies with military politeness, had apologized for the trouble to which he was putting lady Margaret's family, and had received the corresponding assurances that she could not think any thing an inconvenience which brought within the walls of Tillietudlem so distinguished a soldier, and so loyal a servant of his sacred majesty; when, in short, all forms of hospitable and polite ritual had been duly complied with, the Colonel requested permission to receive the report of Bothwell, who was now in attendance, and with whom he spoke apart for a few minutes. Major Bellenden took that opportunity to say to his neice, without the hearing of her grandmother, ' What a trifling foolish girl you are, Edith, to send me by express a letter crammed with nonsense about books and gowns, and to slide the only thing I cared a marvedie about into the postscript.'

' I did not know,' said Edith, hesitating very much, ' whether it would be quite—quite proper for me to'——

' I know what you would say—whether it would
be right to take any interest in a presbyterian. But
I knew this lad's father well.   He was a brave soldier; and, if he was once wrong, he was once right
too: I must commend your caution, Edith, for
having said nothing of this young gentleman's affair to your grandmother—you may rely I shall
not—I will take an opportunity to speak to Claver'se.   Come, my love, they are going to breakfast—Let us follow them.'

CHAPTER XII.

Their breakfast. so warm to be sure they did eat,
A custom in travellers so mighty discreet.   *Prior.*

THE breakfast of lady Margaret Bellenden no
more resembled a modern dejeuné, than the great
stone-hall of Tillietudlem could brook comparison
with a modern drawing-room.   No tea, no coffee,
no variety of rolls, but solid and substantial viands
—the priestly ham, the knightly sirloin, the noble
baron of beef, the princely venison pasty; while
silver flagons, saved with difficulty from the claws
of the Covenanters, now mantled, some with ale,
some with mead, and some with generous wine of
various qualities and descriptions.   The appetites
of the guests were in correspondence to the mag-
nificence and solidity of the preparation—no pid-
dling—no boys' play, but that steady and persevering exercise of the jaws which is best learned by

early morning hours, and by occasional hard commons.

Lady Margaret beheld with delight the cates which she had provided descending with such alacrity into the persons of her honoured guests, and had little occasion to exercise, with respect to any of the company saving Claverhouse himself, the compulsory urgency of pressing to eat, to which, as to the *peine forte et dure*, the ladies of that period were in the custom of subjecting their guests.

But the leader himself, more anxious to pay courtesy to Miss Bellenden, next whom he was placed, than to gratify his appetite, appeared somewhat negligent of the good cheer set before him. Edith heard, without reply, many courtly speeches addressed to her, in a tone of voice of that happy modulation which could alike melt in the low tones of interesting conversation, and rise amid the din of battle, 'loud as a trumpet with a silver sound.' The sense that she was in the presence of the dreaded chief upon whose fiat the fate of Henry Morton must depend—the recollection of the terror and awe which were attached to the very name of the commander, deprived her for some time, not only of the courage to answer, but even of the power of looking upon him. But when, emboldened by the soothing tones of his voice, she lifted her eyes to frame some reply, the person on whom she looked bore, in his appearance at least, none of the terrible attributes in which her apprehensions had arrayed him.

Grahame of Claverhouse was in the prime of life, rather low of stature, and slightly, though elegantly, formed; his gesture, language, and manners, were those of one whose life had been spent among the noble and the gay. His features exhibited even feminine regularity. An oval face, a straight and well-formed nose, dark hazel eyes, a complexion just sufficiently tinged with brown to save it from the charge of effeminacy, a short upper-lip, curved upward like that of a Grecian statue, and slightly shaded by small mustachios of light-brown, joined to a profusion of long curled locks of the same colour, which fell down on each side of his face, contributed to form such a countenance as limners love to paint and ladies to look upon.

The severity of his character, as well as the higher attributes of undaunted and enterprising valour which even his enemies were compelled to admit, lay concealed under an exterior which seemed adapted to the court or the saloon rather than to the field. The same gentleness and gayety of expression which reigned in his features seemed to inspire his actions and gestures; and, on the whole, he was generally esteemed, at first sight, rather qualified to be the votary of pleasure than of ambition. But under this soft exterior was hidden a spirit unbounded in daring and in aspiring, yet cautious and prudent as that of Machiavel himself. Profound in politics, and imbued, of course, with that disregard for individual rights which its intrigues usually generate, this leader was cool and collected in danger, fierce and ardent in pursuing success, careless of death himself, and ruthless in inflicting it upon others. Such are the characters formed in times of civil discord, when the highest qualities, perverted by party spirit, and inflamed by habitual opposition, are too often combined with vices and excesses which deprive them at once of their merit and of their lustre.

In endeavouring to reply to the polite trifles with which Claverhouse accosted her, Edith showed so much confusion, that her grandmother thought it necessary to come to her relief.

'Edith Bellenden,' said the old lady, 'has, from my retired mode of living, seen so little of those of her own sphere, that truly she can hardly frame her speech to suitable answers. A soldier is so rare a sight with us, Colonel Grahame, that unless it be my young Lord Evandale, we have hardly had an opportunity of receiving a gentleman in uniform. And, now I talk of that excellent young nobleman, may I inquire if I was not to have had the honour of seeing him this morning with the regiment?'

'Lord Evandale, madam, was on his march with us,' answered the leader, 'but I was obliged to detach him with a small party to disperse a conventicle of those troublesome scoundrels who have had the impudence to assemble within five miles of my head-quarters.'

'Indeed!' said the old lady; 'that is a height of presumption to which I would have thought no rebellious fanatics would have ventured to aspire. But these are strange times! There is an evil spirit in the land, Colonel Grahame, that excites the vassals of persons of rank to rebel against the very house that holds and feeds them. There was one of my able-bodied men the other day who plainly refused to attend the wappen-schaw at my bidding. Is there no law for such recusancy, Colonel Grahame?'

'I think I could find one,' said Claverhouse, with great composure, ' if your ladyship will inform me of the name and residence of the culprit.'

'His name,' said Lady Margaret, ' is Cuthbert Headrigg; I can say nothing of his domicile, for ye may weel believe, Colonel Grahame, he did not dwell long in Tillietudlem, but was speedily expelled for his contumacy. I wish the lad no ill; but incarceration, or even a few stripes, would be a good example in this neighbourhood. His mother, under whose influence I doubt he acted, is an ancient domestic of this family, which makes me incline to mercy, although,' continued the old lady, looking towards the pictures of her husband and her sons, with which the hall was hung, and heaving, at the same time, a deep sigh, ' I, Colonel Grahame, have in my ain person but little right to compassionate that stubborn and rebellious generation. They have made me a childless widow, and, but for the protection of our sacred sovereign and his gallant soldiers, they would soon deprive me of land and goods, of hearth and altar. Seven of my tenants, whose joint rent-mail may mount to well nigh a hundred merks, have already refused to pay either cess or rent, and had the assurance to tell my steward that they would acknowledge neither king nor landlord but who should have taken the Covenant.'

'I will take a course with them—that is, with your ladyship's permission,' answered Claverhouse; ' it would ill become me to neglect the support of lawful authority when it is lodged in such worthy hands as that of Lady Margaret Bellenden. But I must needs say this country grows worse and worse daily, and reduces me to the necessity of taking

measures with the recusants that are much more
consonant with my duty than with my inclinations.
And, speaking of this, I must not forget that I have
to thank your ladyship for the hospitality you have
been pleased to extend to a party of mine who have
brought in a prisoner, charged with having resetted
the murdering villain, Balfour of Burley.'

' The house of Tillietudlem,' answered the lady,
' hath ever been open to the servants of his majesty,
and I hope that the stones of it will no longer rest
on each other when it surceases to be as much at
their command as at ours. And this reminds me,
Colonel Grahame, that the gentleman who commands the party can hardly be said to be in his proper place in the army, considering whose blood flows
in his veins; and if I might flatter myself that any
thing would be granted to my request, I would presume to entreat that he might be promoted on some
favourable opportunity.'

' Your ladyship means Serjeant Francis Stuart,
whom we call Bothwell?' said Claverhouse, smiling.
' The truth is, he is a little too rough in the country,
and has not been uniformly so amenable to discipline as the rules of the service require. But to in-
struct me how to oblige Lady Margaret Bellenden
is to lay down the law to me—Bothwell,' he continued, addressing the serjeant, who just then appeared at the door, ' go kiss Lady Margaret Bellenden's hand, who interests herself in your promotion, and you shall have a commission the first va-
cancy.'

Bothwell went through the salutation in the manner prescribed, but not without evident marks of
haughty reluctance, and, when he had done so, said

aloud, ' To kiss a lady's hand can never disgrace a gentleman; but I would not kiss a man's, save the king's, to be made a general.'

' You hear him,' said Claverhouse, smiling, ' there's the rock he splits upon; he cannot forget his pedigree.'

' I know, my noble colonel,' said Bothwell in the same tone, ' that *you* will not forget your promise; and then, perhaps, you may permit *Cornet* Stuart to have some recollection of his grandfather, though the *serjeant* must forget him.'

' Enough of this, sir,' said Claverhouse, in the tone of command which was familiar to him, ' and let me know what you came to report to me just now.'

' My Lord Evandale and his party have halted on the high-road with some prisoners,' said Bothwell.

' My Lord Evandale?' said Lady Margaret. ' Surely, Colonel Grahame, you will permit him to honour me with his society, and to take his poor disjune here, especially considering, that even his most sacred majesty did not pass the Tower of Tillietudlem without halting to partake of some refreshment.'

As this was the third time in the course of the conversation that Lady Margaret had adverted to this distinguished event, Colonel Grahame, as speedily as politeness would permit, took advantage of the first pause to interrupt the farther progress of the narrative, by saying, ' We are already too numerous a party of guests; but as I know what Lord Evandale will suffer (looking towards Edith) if deprived of the pleasure which we enjoy, I will run

the risk of overburdening your ladyship's hospitality.——Bothwell, let Lord Evandale know that Lady
Margaret Bellenden requests the honour of his
company.'

'And let Harrison take care,' added Lady Margaret, 'that the people and their horses are suitably
seen to.'

Edith's heart sprung to her lips during this conversation, for it instantly occurred to her, that,
through her influence over Lord Evandale, she might
find some means of releasing Morton from his present state of danger, in case her uncle's intercession
with Claverhouse should prove ineffectual. At any
other time, she would have been much averse to
exert this influence; for, however inexperienced in
the world, her native delicacy taught her the advantage which a beautiful young woman gives to a
young man when she permits him to lay her under
an obligation. And she would have been the farther
disinclined to request any favour of Lord Evandale, because the voice of the gossips in Clydesdale
had, for reasons hereafter to be made known, assigned him to her as a suitor, and because she
could not disguise from herself that very little en-
couragement was necessary to realize conjectures
which had hitherto no foundation. This was the
more to be dreaded, that, in the case of Lord Evandale's making a formal declaration, he had every
chance of being supported by the influence of Lady
Margaret and her other friends, and that she would
have nothing to oppose to their solicitations and authority, except a predilection, to avow which she
knew would be equally dangerous and unavailing. She
determined, therefore, to wait the issue of her un-

cle's intercession, and, should it fail, which she conjectured she should soon learn, either from the looks or language of the open-hearted veteran, she would then, as a last effort, make use in Morton's favour of her interest with Lord Evandale. Her mind did not long remain in suspense on the subject of her uncle's application.

Major Bellenden, who had done the honours of the table, laughing and chatting with the military guests who were at that end of the board, was now, by the conclusion of the repast, at liberty to leave his station, and accordingly took an opportunity to approach Claverhouse, requesting from his niece, at the same time, the honour of a particular introduction. As his name and character were well known, the two military men met with expressions of mutual regard, and Edith, with a beating heart, saw her aged relative withdraw from the company, together with his new acquaintance, into a recess formed by one of the arched windows of the hall. She watched their conference with eyes almost dazzled by the eagerness of suspense, and, with observation rendered more acute by the internal agony of her mind, could guess, from the pantomimic gestures which accompanied the conversation, the progress and fate of the intercession in behalf of Henry Morton.

- The first expression of the countenance of Claverhouse betokened that open and willing courtesy, which, ere it requires to know the nature of the favour asked, seems to say, how happy the party will be to confer an obligation on the suppliant. But as the conversation proceeded, the brow of that officer became darker and more severe, and his features, though still retaining the expression of the most perfect politeness, assumed, at least to Edith's terrified imagination, a harsh and inexorable character. His lip was now compressed as if with impatience; now curled slightly upward as if in civil contempt of the arguments urged by major Bellenden. The language of her uncle, as far as expressed in his manner, appeared to be that of earnest intercession, urged with all the affectionate simplicity of his character, as well as with the weight which his age and reputation entitled him to use. But it seemed to have little impression upon colonel Grahame, who soon changed his posture, as if about to cut short the major's importunity, and to break up their conference with a courtly expression of regret, calculated to accompany a positive refusal of the request solicited. This movement brought them so near Edith, that she could distinctly hear Claverhouse say, ' It cannot be, major Bellenden; lenity, in this case, is altogether beyond the bounds of my commission, though in any thing else I am so heartily desirous to oblige you.——And here comes Evandale with news, as I think. What tidings do you bring us, Evandale?' he continued, addressing the young lord, who now entered in complete uniform, but with his dress disordered, and his boots spattered as if by riding hard.

' Unpleasant news, sir,' was his reply. ' A large body of whigs are in arms among the hills, and have broken out into actual rebellion. They have publickly burnt the Act of Supremacy, that which established episcopacy, that for observing the martyrdom of Charles I, and some others, and have declared their intention to remain together in arms for furthering the covenanted work of reformation.'

This unexpected intelligence struck a sudden and painful surprise into the minds of all who heard it, excepting Claverhouse.

'Unpleasant news call you them?' replied colonel Grahame, his dark eyes flashing fire, 'they are the best I have heard these six months. Now that the scoundrels are drawn into a body we will make short work with them. When the adder crawls into daylight,' he added, striking the heel of his boot upon the floor, as if in the act of crushing a noxious reptile, 'I can trample him to death; he is only safe when he remains lurking in his den or morass.—— Where are these knaves?' he continued, addressing lord Evandale.

'About ten miles off among the mountains, at a place called Loudon-hill,' was the young nobleman's reply. 'I dispersed the conventicle against which you sent me, and made prisoner an old trumpeter of rebellion, who was in the act of exhorting his hearers to rise and be doing in the good cause, as well as one or two of his hearers who seemed to be particularly insolent; and from some country people and scouts I learned what I now tell you.'

'What may be their strength?' asked his commander.

'Probably a thousand men, but accounts differ widely.'

'Then,' said Claverhouse, 'it is time for us to be up and be doing also—Bothwell, bid them sound to horse.'

Bothwell, who, like the war-horse of scripture, snuffed the battle afar off, hastened to give orders to six negroes, in white dresses richly laced, and having massive silver collars and armlets. These sable functionaries acted as trumpeters, and speedily made the castle and the woods around it ring with their summons.

'Must you then leave us?' said Lady Margaret, her heart sinking under recollection of former unhappy times; 'had ye no better send to learn the force of the rebels?—O, how many a fair face hae I heard these fearfu' sounds call away frae the Tower of Tillietudlem, that my auld e'en were ne'er to see return to it!'

'It is impossible for me to stop,' said Claverhouse; 'there are rogues enough in this country to make the rebels five times their strength, if they are not checked at once.'

'Many,' said Evandale, 'are flocking to them already, and they give out that they expect a strong body of the indulged presbyterians, headed by young Milnwood, as they call him, the son of the famous old round-head, Colonel Silas Morton.'

This speech produced a very different effect upon the hearers. Edith almost sunk from her seat with terror, while Claverhouse darted a glance of sarcastic triumph at major Bellenden, which seemed to imply—'You see what are the principles of the young man you are pleading for.'

'It's a lie—it's a d—d lie of these rascally fanatics,' said the major, hastily. 'I will answer for Henry Morton as I would for my own son. He is a lad of as good church-principles as any gentleman in the life-guards. I mean no offence to any one. He has gone to church service with me fifty times, and I never heard him miss one of the responses in my life. Edith Bellenden can bear witness to it as

well as I. He always read on the same Prayer-book
with her, and could look out the lessons as well as
the curate himself. Call him up; let him be heard
for himself.'

'There can be no harm in that,' said Claverhouse,
'whether he be innocent or guilty.——Major Allan,'
he said, turning to the officer next in command,
'take a guide, and lead the regiment forward to
Loudon-hill by the best and shortest road. Move
steadily, and do not blow the horses; Lord Evandale and I will overtake you in a quarter of an hour.
Leave Bothwell with a party to bring up the prisoners.'

Allan bowed, and left the apartment, with all the
officers, excepting Claverhouse and the young nobleman. In a few minutes the sound of the military
music and the clashing of hoofs announced that the
horsemen were leaving the Castle. The sounds were
presently heard only at intervals, and soon died
away entirely.

While Claverhouse endeavoured to sooth the terrors of Lady Margaret, and to reconcile the veteran
Major to his opinion of Morton, Evandale, getting
the better of that conscious shyness which renders
an ingenuous youth diffident in approaching the object of his affections, drew near to Miss Bellenden,
and accosted her in a tone of mingled respect and
interest.

'We are to leave you,' he said, taking her hand,
which he pressed with much emotion——'to leave
you for a scene which is not without its dangers.
Farewell, dear Miss Bellenden;——let me say for the
first, and perhaps the last time, dear Edith. We part
in circumstances so singular as may excuse some so-

lemnity in bidding farewell to one, whom I have known so long, and whom I—respect so highly.'

The manner differing from the words, seemed to express a feeling much deeper and more agitating than was conveyed in the phrase he made use of. It was not in woman to be utterly insensible to his modest and deep-felt expression of tenderness. Although borne down by the misfortunes and imminent danger of the man she loved, Edith was touched by the hopeless and reverential passion of the gallant youth, who now took leave of her to rush into dangers of no ordinary description.

' I hope—I sincerely trust,' she said, ' there is no danger. I hope there is no occasion for this solemn ceremonial—that these hasty insurgents will be dispersed rather by fear than force, and that Lord Evandale will speedily return to be what he must always be, the dear and valued friend of all in this castle.'

' Of *all?*' he repeated, with a melancholy emphasis upon the word. ' But be it so—whatever is near you is dear and valued to me, and I value their approbation accordingly. Of our success I am not sanguine. Our numbers are so few, that I dare not hope for so speedy, so bloodless, or so safe an end of this unhappy disturbance. These men are enthusiastic, resolute, and desperate, and have leaders not altogether unskilled in military matters. I cannot help thinking that the impetuosity of our Colonel is hurrying us against them rather prematurely. But there are few that have less reason to shun danger than I have.'

Edith had now the opportunity she wished to bespeak the young nobleman's intercession and protection for Henry Morton, and it seemed the only remaining channel of interest by which he could be rescued from impending destruction.   Yet she felt at that moment as if, in doing so, she was abusing the partiality and confidence of the lover, whose heart was as open before her as if his tongue had made an express declaration.   Could she with honour engage Lord Evandale in the service of a rival? or could she with prudence make him any request, or lay herself under any obligation to him, without affording ground for hopes which she could never realize? But the moment was too urgent for hesitation, or even for those explanations with which her request might otherwise have been qualified.

' I will but dispose of this young fellow,' said Claverhouse, from the other side of the hall, ' and then, Lord Evandale—I am sorry to interrupt again your conversation—but then we must mount.— Bothwell, why do you not bring up the prisoner? and, hark ye, let two files load their carabines.'

In these words, Edith conceived she heard the death-warrant of her lover.   She instantly broke through the restraint which had hitherto kept her silent.

' My Lord Evandale,' she said, ' this young gentlemen is a particular friend of my uncle's —your interest must be great with your colonel—let me request your intercession in his favour—it will confer on my uncle a lasting obligation.'

' You over-rate my interest, Miss Bellenden,' said Lord Evandale, ' I have been often unsuccessful in such applications, when I have made them on the mere score of humanity.'

' Yet try once again for my uncle's sake.'

' And why not for your own?' said Lord Evandale. ' Will you not allow me to think I am obliging *you* personally in this matter?—Are you so diffident of an old friend that you will not allow him even the satisfaction of thinking that he is gratifying your wishes?'

' Surely—surely,' replied Edith; ' you will oblige me infinitely—I am interested in the young gentleman on my uncle's account—Lose no time, for God's sake!'

She became bolder and more urgent in her entreaties, for she heard the steps of the soldiers who were entering with their prisoner.

' By Heaven! then,' said Evandale, ' he shall not die, if I should die in his place!—But will not you,' he said, resuming the hand, which in the hurry of her spirits she had not courage to withdraw, ' will not you grant me one suit, in return for my zeal in your service?'

' Any thing you can ask, my Lord Evandale, that sisterly affection can give.'

' And is this all,' he continued, ' all you cant grant to my affection living, or my memory when dead?'

' Do not speak thus, my lord,' said Edith, ' you distress me, and do injustice to yourself. There is no friend I esteem more highly, or to whom I would more readily grant every mark of regard—providing—But'——

A deep sigh made her turn her head suddenly, ere she had well uttered the last word; and, as she hesitated how to frame the exception with which she meant to close the sentence, she became instantly aware she had been overheard by Morton, who,

heavily ironed and guarded by soldiers, was now
passing behind her in order to be presented to Claverhouse. As their eyes met each other, the sad and
reproachful expression of Morton's glance seemed
to imply that he had partially heard, and altogether
misinterpreted, the conversation which had just
passed. There wanted but this to complete Edith's
distress and confusion. Her blood, which rushed to
her brow, made a sudden revulsion to her heart,
and left her as pale as death. This change did not
escape the attention of Evandale, whose quick
glance easily discovered that there was between the
prisoner and the object of his own attachment, some
singular and uncommon connexion. He resigned
the hand of Miss Bellenden, again surveyed the
prisoner with more attention, again looked at Edith,
and plainly observed the confusion which she could
no longer conceal.

'This,' he said, after a moment's gloomy silence,
'is, I believe, the young gentleman who gained the
prize at the shooting-match.'

'I am not sure,' hesitated Edith—'yet—I rather
think not,' scarce knowing what she replied.

'It *is* he,' said Evandale, decidedly; 'I know him
well. A victor,' he continued, somewhat haughtily,
'ought to have interested a fair spectator more
deeply.'

He then turned from Edith, and advancing towards the table at which Claverhouse now placed
himself, stood at a little distance, resting on his
sheathed broadsword, a silent, but not an uncon-
cerned, spectator of that which passed.

CHAPTER XIII.

O, my Lord, beware of jealousy!   *Othello.*

To explain the deep effect which the few broken passages of the conversation we have detailed, made upon the unfortunate prisoner by whom they were overheard, it is necessary to say something of his previous state of mind, and of the origin of his connection with Edith.

Henry Morton was one of those gifted characters which possess a force of talent unsuspected by the owner himself. He had inherited from his father an undaunted courage, and a firm and uncompromising detestation of oppression, whether in politics or religion. But his enthusiasm was unsullied by fanatical zeal, and unleavened by the sourness of the puritanical spirit. From these his mind had been freed, partly by the active exertions of his own excellent understanding, partly by frequent and long visits at major Bellenden's, where he had an opportunity of meeting with many guests whose conversation taught him, that goodness and worth were not limited to those of any single form of religious observance.

The base parsimony of his uncle had thrown many obstacles in the way of his education; but he had so far improved the opportunities which offered themselves, that his instructors as well as his friends were surprised at his progress under such disadvantages. Still, however, the current of his soul was frozen by a sense of dependence, of poverty, above all, of an imperfect and limited education.

These feelings impressed him with a diffidence and reserve which effectually concealed from all but very intimate friends, the extent of talent and the firmness of character, which we have stated him to be possessed of. The circumstances of the times had added to this reserve an air of indecision and of indifference; for, being attached to neither of the factions which divided the kingdom, he passed for dull, insensible, and uninfluenced by the feeling of religion or of patriotism. No conclusion, however, could be more unjust: and the reasons of the neutrality which he had hitherto professed had root in very different and most praise-worthy motives. He had formed few congenial ties with those who were the objects of persecution, and was disgusted alike by their narrow-minded and selfish party-spirit, their gloomy fanaticism, their abhorrent condemnation of all elegant studies or innocent exercises, and the envenomed rancour of their political hatred. But his mind was still more revolted by the tyrannical and oppressive conduct of the government, the misrule, license, and brutality of the soldiery, the executions on the scaffold, the slaughters in the open field, the free quarters and exactions imposed by military law, which placed the lives and fortunes of a free people on a level with Asiatic slaves. Condemning, therefore, each party as its excesses fell under his eyes, disgusted with the sight of evils which he had no means of alleviating, and hearing alternate complaints and exultations with which he could not sympathise, he would long ere this have left Scotland had it not been for his attachment to Edith Bellenden.

The earlier meeting of these young people had been at Charnwood, when major Bellenden, who was as free from suspicion on such occasions as Uncle Toby himself, had encouraged their keeping each other constant company without entertaining any apprehension of the natural consequences. Love, as usual in such cases, borrowed the name of friendship, used her language, and claimed her privileges. When Edith Bellenden was recalled to her mother's castle, it was astonishing by what singular and recurring accidents she often met young Morton in her sequestered walks, especially considering the distance of their places of abode. Yet it somehow happened that she never expressed the surprise which the frequency of these rencontres ought naturally to have excited, and that their intercourse assumed gradually a more delicate character, and their meetings began to wear the air of appointments. Books, drawings, letters, were exchanged between them, and every trifling commission, given or executed, gave rise to a new correspondence. Love indeed was not yet mentioned between them by name, but each knew the situation of their own bosom, and could not but guess at that of the other. Unable to desist from an intercourse which possessed such charms for them both, yet trembling for its too probable consequences, it had been continued without specific explanation until now, when fate appeared to have taken the conclusion into its own hands.

It followed, as a consequence of this state of things, as well as of the diffidence of Morton's disposition at this period, that his confidence in Edith's return of his affection had its occasional cold fits. Her situation was in every respect so superior

his own, her worth so eminent, her accomplishments
so many, her face so beautiful, and her manners so
bewitching, that he could not but entertain fears that
some suitor more favoured than himself by fortune,
and more acceptable to Edith's family than he durst
hope to be, might step in between him and the object of her affections. Common rumour had raised
up such a rival in lord Evandale, whom birth, fortune, connections, and political principles, as well
as his frequent visits at Tillietudlem, and his attendance upon lady Bellenden and her niece at all public places, naturally pointed out as a candidate for
her favour. It frequently and inevitably happened
that engagements to which lord Evandale was a
party, interfered with the meeting of the lovers, and
Henry could not but mark that Edith either studi-
ously avoided speaking of the young nobleman, or
did so with obvious reserve and hesitation.

These symptoms, which, in fact, arose from the
delicacy of her own feelings towards Morton himself, were misconstrued by his diffident temper, and
the jealousy which they excited was fermented by
the occasional observations of Jenny Dennison. This
true-bred serving-damsel was, in her own person, a
complete country coquette, and when she had no opportunity of teazing her own lovers, used to take
some occasional opportunity to torment her young
lady's. This arose from no ill-will to Henry Morton, who, both on her mistress's account and his own
handsome form and countenance, stood high in her
esteem. But then lord Evandale was also handsome; he was liberal far beyond what Morton's
means could afford, and he was a lord, moreover;
and, if Miss Edith Bellenden should accept his

hand, she would become a baron's lady, and what was more, little Jenny Dennison, whom the awful housekeeper at Tillietudlem huffed about at her pleasure, would be then Mrs. Dennison, lady Evandale's own woman, or perhaps her ladyship's lady-in-waiting. The impartiality of Jenny Dennison, therefore, did not, like that of Mrs. Quickly, extend to a wish that both the handsome suitors could wed her young lady; for it must be owned that the scale of her regard was depressed in favour of lord Evandale, and her wishes in his favour took many shapes extremely tormenting to Morton; being now expressed as a friendly caution, now as an article of intelligence, and anon as a merry jest, but always tending to confirm the idea, that, sooner or later, his romantic intercourse with her young mistress must have a close, and that Edith Bellenden would, in spite of summer walks beneath the greenwood-tree, exchange of verses, of drawings, and of books, end in becoming lady Evandale.

These hints coincided so exactly with the very point of his own suspicions and fears, that Morton was not long of feeling that jealousy which every one has felt who has truly loved, but to which those are most liable whose love is crossed by the want of friends' consent, or some other envious impediment of fortune. Edith herself, unwittingly, and in the generosity of her own frank nature, contributed to the error into which her lover was in danger of falling. Their conversation once chanced to turn upon some late excesses committed by the soldiery on an occasion when it was said (inaccurately however) that the party was commanded by lord Evandale. Edith, as true in friendship as in love, was somewhat hurt at the severe strictures which escaped from Morton upon this occasion, and which, perhaps, were not the less*strongly expressed on account of their supposed rivalry. She entered into lord Evandale's defence with such spirit as hurt Morton to the very soul, and afforded no small delight to Jenny Dennison, the usual companion of their walks. Edith perceived her error, and endeavoured to remedy it; but the impression was not so easily erazed, and it had no small effect in inducing her lover to form that resolution of going abroad, which was disappointed in the manner we have already mentioned.

The visit which he received from Edith during his confinement, the deep and devoted interest which she had expressed in his fate, ought of themselves to have dispelled his suspicions; yet, ingenious in tormenting himself, even this he thought might be imputed to anxious friendship, or, at most, to a temporary partiality, which would probably soon give way to circumstances, the entreaties of her friends, the authority of lady Margaret, and the assiduities of lord Evandale.

'And to what do I owe it,' he said, 'that I cannot stand up like a man, and plead my interest in her ere I am thus cheated out of it?—to what, but to the accursed tyranny which afflicts at once our bodies, souls, estates, and affections! And is it to one of the pensioned cut-throats of this oppressive government that I must yield my pretensions to Edith Bellenden?—I will not, by Heaven!—It is a just punishment on me for being dead to public wrongs, that they have visited me with their injuries in a point where they can be least brooked or borne.'

As these stormy resolutions boiled in his bosom, and while he ran over the various kinds of insult and injury which he had sustained in his own cause and in that of his country, Bothwell entered the tower, followed by two dragoons, one of whom carried handcuffs.

' You must follow me, young man,' said he, ' but first we must put you in trim.'

' In trim!' said Morton, ' What do you mean?'

' Why, we must put on these rough bracelets. I durst not—nay, d—n it I *durst* do any thing—but I *would* not for three hours plunder of a stormed town bring a whig before my colonel without his being ironed. Come, come, young man, never look sulky about it.'

He advanced to put on the irons; but, seizing the oaken-seat upon which he had rested, Morton threatened to dash out the brains of the first who should approach him.

' I should manage you in a moment, my youngster,' said Bothwell, ' but I had rather you would strike sail quietly.'

Here indeed he spoke the truth, not from either fear or reluctance to adopt force, but because he dreaded the consequences of a noisy scuffle, through which it might probably be discovered that he had, contrary to express orders, suffered his prisoner to pass the night without being properly secured.

' You had better be prudent,' he continued, in a tone which he meant to be conciliatory, ' and don't spoil your own sport. They say here in the castle that lady Margaret's niece is immediately to marry our young captain, lord Evandale. I saw them close together in the hall yonder, and I heard her ask him to intercede for your pardon. She looked so devilish handsome and kind upon him, that on my soul—but what the devil's the matter with you?— You are as pale as a sheet—Will you have some brandy?'

' Miss Bellenden ask my life of lord Evandale?' said the prisoner, faintly.

' Ay, ay; there's no friend like the women—their interest carries all in court and camp.—Come, you are reasonable now—Ay, I thought you would come round.'

Here he employed himself in putting on the fetters, against which, Morton, thunderstruck by this intelligence, no longer offered the least resistance.

' My life begged of him, and by her!—ay—ay— put on the irons—my limbs shall not refuse to bear what has entered into my very soul—My life begged by Edith, and begged of Evandale!'

' Ay, and he has power to grant it too,' said Bothwell—' He can do more with the colonel than any man in the regiment.'

And, as he spoke, he and his party led their prisoner towards the hall. In passing behind the seat of Edith the unfortunate prisoner heard enough, as he conceived, of the broken expressions which passed between Edith and lord Evandale to confirm all that the soldier had told him. That moment made a singular and instantaneous revolution in his character. The depth of despair to which his love and fortunes were reduced, the peril in which his life appeared to stand, the transference of Edith's affections, her intercession in his favour, which rendered

her fickleness yet more galling, seemed to destroy
every feeling for which he had hitherto lived, but,
at the same time, awakened those which had hitherto been smothered by passions more gentle though
more selfish.   Desperate himself, he determined to
support the rights of his country, insulted in his
person. His character was for the moment as effectually changed as the appearance of a villa, which,
from being the abode of domestic quiet and happiness, is, by the sudden intrusion of an armed force,
converted into a formidable post of defence.

We have already said that he cast upon Edith
one glance in which reproach was mingled with
sorrow, as if to bid her farewell for ever; his next
motion was to walk firmly to the table at which
Colonel Grahame was seated.

' By what right is it, sir,' said he firmly, and without waiting till he was questioned,—' By what right
is it that these soldiers have dragged me from my
family, and put fetters on the limbs of a free man?'

' By my commands,' answered Claverhouse; ' and
I now lay my commands on you to be silent and
hear my questions.'

' I will not,' replied Morton, in a determined
tone, while his boldness seemed to electrify all
around him. ' I will know whether I am in lawful
custody, and before a civil magistrate, ere the charter of my country shall be forfeited in my person.'

' A pretty springald this, upon my honour!' said
Claverhouse.

' Are you mad?' said Major Bellenden to his
young friend. ' For God's sake, Henry Morton,'
he continued, in a tone between a rebuke and en-

treaty, ' remember you are speaking to one of his majesty's officers high in the service.'

' It is for that very reason, sir,' returned Henry, firmly, ' that I desire to know what right he has to detain me without a legal warrant. Were he a civil officer of the law, I should know my duty was submission.'

' Your friend here,' said Claverhouse to the veteran, coolly, ' is one of those scrupulous gentlemen, who, like the madman in the play, will not tie his cravat without the warrant of Mr. Justice Overdo; but I will let him see, before we part, that my shoulder-knot is as legal a badge of authority as the mace of the Justiciary. So, waiving this discussion, you will be pleased, young man, to tell me directly when you saw Balfour of Burley.'

' As I know no right you have to ask such a question, I decline replying to it.'

' You confessed to my serjeant,' said Claverhouse, ' that you saw and entertained him, knowing him to be an inter-communed traitor, why are you not so frank with me?'

' Because,' replied the prisoner, ' I presume you are, from education, taught to understand the rights upon which you seem disposed to trample, and I am willing you should be aware there are yet Scotsmen who can assert the liberties of Scotland.'

' And these supposed rights you would vindicate with your sword, I presume?' said Colonel Grahame.

' Were I armed as you are, and we were alone upon a hill-side, you should not ask me the question twice.'

' It is quite enough,' answered Claverhouse, calmly; ' your language corresponds with all I have heard of you;—but you are the son of a soldier, though a rebellious one, and you shall not die the death of a dog; I will save you that indignity.'

' Die in what manner I may,' replied Morton, ' I will die like the son of a brave man; and the ignominy you mention shall remain with those who shed innocent blood.'

' Make your peace, then, with Heaven in five minutes space.—Bothwell, lead him down to the court-yard, and draw up your party.'

The appalling nature of this conversation, and of its result, struck the silence of horror into all but the speakers. But now those who stood round broke forth into clamour and expostulation. Old Lady Margaret, who, with all the prejudices of rank and party, had not laid aside the feelings of her sex, was loud in her intercession.

' O, Colonel Grahame,' she exclaimed, ' spare his young blood! Leave him to the law—do not repay my hospitality by shedding men's blood on the threshold of my doors!'

' Colonel Grahame,' said Major Bellenden, ' you must answer this violence. Don't think, though I am old and feckless, that my friend's son shall be murdered before my eyes with impunity. I can find friends that shall make you answer it.'

' Be satisfied, Major Bellenden, I will answer it,' replied Claverhouse, totally unmoved; ' and you madam, might spare me the pain of resisting this passionate intercession for a traitor, when you consider the noble blood your own house has lost by such as he is.'

' Colonel Grahame,' answered the lady, her aged frame trembling with anxiety, ' I leave vengeance to God, who calls it his own. The shedding of this young man's blood will not call back the lives that were dear to me; and how can it comfort me to think that there has maybe been another widowed mother made childless, like mysel, by a deed done at my very door-stane.'

' This is stark madness,' said Claverhouse; ' I *must* do my duty to church and state. Here are a thousand villains hard by in open rebellion, and you ask me to pardon a young fanatic who is enough of himself to set a whole kingdom in a blaze! It cannot be—remove him, Bothwell.'

She who was most interested in this dreadful decision had twice strove to speak, but her voice had totally failed her; her mind refused to suggest words and her tongue to utter them. She now sprung up and attempted to rush forward, but her strength gave way, and she would have fallen flat upon the pavement had she not been caught by her attendant.

' Help,' cried Jenny,—' Help for God's sake! my young lady is dying.'

At this exclamation, Evandale, who during the preceding part of the scene, had stood motionless, leaning upon his sword, now stepped forward, and said to his commanding-officer, ' Colonel Grahame, before proceeding in this matter, will you speak a word with me in private?'

Claverhouse looked surprised, but instantly rose and withdrew with the young nobleman into a recess, where the following brief dialogue passed between them:

' I think I need not remind you, colonel, that
when our family interest was of service to you last
year in that affair in the privy council, you considered yourself as laid under some obligation to us?'

' Certainly, my dear Evandale;' answered Claverhouse, ' I am not a man who forgets such debts; you
will delight me by showing how I can evince my
gratitude.'

' I will hold the debt cancelled if you will spare
this young man's life.'

' Evandale,' replied Grahame, in great surprise,
' you are mad—absolutely mad—what interest can
you have in this young spawn of an old roundhead?
—His father was positively the most dangerous man
in all Scotland, cool, resolute, soldierly, and inflex-
ible in his cursed principles. His son seems his
very model; you cannot conceive the mischief he
may do—I know mankind, Evandale—were he an
insignificant, fanatical, country booby, do you think
I would have refused such a trifle as his life to lady
Margaret and this family? But this is a lad of fire,
zeal, and education—and these knaves want but such
a leader to direct their blind enthusiastic hardiness.
I mention this not as refusing your request, but to
make you fully aware of the possible consequences—
I will never evade a promise, or refuse to return
an obligation—If you ask his life, he shall have it.'

' Keep him close prisoner,' answered Evandale,
' but do not be surprised if I persist in requesting
you will not put him to death. I have most urgent
reasons for what I ask.'

' Be it so then,' replied Grahame;—' but, young
man, should you wish in your future life to rise to
eminence in the service of your king and country,

let it be your first task to subject to the public interest, and to the discharge of your duty, your private passions, affections, and feelings. These are not times to sacrifice to the dotage of graybeards, or the tears of silly women, the measures of salutary severity, which the dangers around compel us to adopt. And remember, that if I now yield this point, in compliance with your urgency, my present concession must exempt me from future solicitations of the same nature.'

He then stepped forward to the table, and bent his eyes keenly on Morton, as if to observe what effect the pause of awful suspense between death and life, which seemed to freeze the by-standers with horror, should produce upon the prisoner himself. Morton maintained a degree of firmness, which nothing but a mind which had nothing left on earth to love, or to hope, could have supported at such a crisis.

'You see him,' said Claverhouse, in a half whisper to Lord Evandale, 'he is tottering on the verge between time and eternity, a situation more appalling than the most hideous certainty; yet his is the only cheek unblenched, the only eye that is calm, the only heart that keeps its usual time, the only nerves that are not quivering. Look at him well, Evandale—If that man heads an army of rebels, you will have much to answer for on account of this morning's work.' He then said aloud, 'Young man, your life is for the present safe, through the intercession of your friends.—Remove him, Bothwell, and let him be properly guarded and brought along with the other prisoners.'

'If my life,' said Morton, stung with the idea that he owed his respite to the intercession of a favoured rival, 'if my life be granted at Lord Evandale's request'——

'Take the prisoner away, Bothwell,' said Colonel Grahame, interrupting him; 'I have neither time to make nor to hear fine speeches.'

Bothwell forced off Morton, saying, as he conducted him into the court-yard, 'Have you three lives in your pocket, besides the one in your body, my lad, that you can afford to let your tongue run away with them at this rate? Come, come, I'll take care to keep you out of the colonel's way, for egad you will not be five minutes with him before the next tree or the next ditch will be the word. So, come along to your companions in bondage.'

So saying, the sergeant, who, in his rude manner, did not altogether want sympathy for a gallant young man, hurried Morton down to the court-yard, where three other prisoners (two men and a woman) who had been taken by Lord Evandale, remained under an escort of dragoons.

Mean time, Claverhouse took his leave of Lady Margaret. But it was difficult for the good lady to forgive his neglect of her intercession.

'I have thought till now,' she said, 'that the Tower of Tillietudlem might have been a place of succour to those that are ready to perish, even if they werena sae deserving as they should have been—but I see auld fruit has little savour—our suffering and our services have been of an ancient date.'

'They are never to be forgotten by me, let me assure your ladyship,' said Claverhouse. 'Nothing but what seemed my sacred duty could make me

hesitate to grant a favour requested by you and the
Major. Come, my good lady, let me hear you say
you have forgiven me, and, as I return to-night, I
will bring a drove of two hundred whigs with me,
and pardon fifty head of them for your sake.

'I shall be happy to hear of your success, Colonel,' said Major Bellenden; 'but take an old soldier's advice, and spare blood when battle's over—
and once more let me request to enter bail for young
Morton.'

'We will settle that when I return,' said Claverhouse. 'Meanwhile, be assured his life shall be
safe.'

During this conversation, Evandale looked anxiously around for Edith; but the precaution of Jenny
Dennison had occasioned her mistress being transported to her own apartment.

Slowly and heavily he obeyed the impatient summons of Claverhouse, who, after taking a courteous
leave of Lady Margaret and the Major, had hastened
to the court-yard. The prisoners with their guards
were already on their march, and the officers with
their escort mounted and followed. All pressed forward to overtake the main body, as it was supposed they would come in sight of the enemy in not
more than two hours.

CHAPTER XIV.

My hounds may a' rin masterless,
   My hawks may fly frae tree to tree,
My lord may grip my vassal lands,
   For there again maun I never be!   *Old Ballad.*

WE left Morton, along with three companions in
captivity, travelling in the custody of a small body
of soldiers who formed the rear-guard of the column under the command of Claverhouse, and were
immediately under the charge of serjeant Bothwell.
Their route lay towards the hills in which the insurgent presbyterians were reported to be in arms.
They had not prosecuted their march a quarter of
a mile ere Claverhouse and Evandale gallopped
past them, followed by their orderly-men, in order
to take their proper places in the column which
preceded them. No sooner were they past than
Bothwell halted the body which he commanded,
and disencumbered Morton of his irons.

'King's blood must keep word,' said the dragoon.
'I promised you should be civilly treated so far as
rested with me.—Here, Corporal Inglis, let this
gentleman ride alongside of the other young fellow
who is prisoner; and you may permit them to converse together at their pleasure, under their breath,
but take care they are guarded by two files with
loaded carabines. If they attempt an escape, blow
their brains out.—You cannot call that using you
uncivilly,' he continued, addressing himself to Morton, 'it's the rules of war; you know.—And, Inglis,
couple up the parson and the old woman, they are

fittest company for each other, d——n me; a single file may guard them well enough. If they speak a word of cant or fanatical nonsence, let them have a strapping with a shoulder belt. There's some hope of choking a silenced parson; if he is not allowed to hold forth, his own treason will burst him.'

Having made this arrangment, Bothwell placed himself at the head of the party, and Inglis, with six dragoons, brought up the rear. The whole then set forward at a trot, with the purpose of overtaking the main-body of the regiment.

Morton, overwhelmed with a complication of feelings, was totally indifferent to the various arrangements made for his secure custody, and even to the relief afforded him by his release from the fetters. He experienced that blank and waste of the heart which follows the hurricane of passion, and, no longer supported by the pride and conscious rectitude which dictated his answers to Claverhouse, he surveyed with deep dejection the glades through which he travelled, each turning of which had something to remind him of past happiness and disappointed hope. The eminence which they now ascended was that from which he used first and last to behold the ancient tower when approaching or retiring from it, and, it is needless to add, that there he was wont to pause, and gaze with a lover's delight on the battlements, which, rising at a distance out of the lofty wood, indicated the dwelling of her, whom he either hoped soon to meet or had recently parted from. Instinctively he turned his head back to take a last look of a scene formerly so dear to him, and no less instinctively he heaved a deep sigh. It was echoed by a loud groan from his companion in

misfortune, whose eyes, moved perchance, by similar reflections, had taken the same direction. This
indication of sympathy, on the part of the captive,
was uttered in a tone more coarse than sentimen-
tal; it was, however, the expression of a grieved
spirit, and so far corresponded with the sigh of
Morton. In turning their heads their eyes met, and
Morton recognised the stolid countenance of Cuddie Headrigg, bearing a rueful expression, in which
sorrow for his own lot was mixed with sympathy
for the situation of his companion.

' Hegh, sirs!' was the expression of the ci-divant
ploughman of the mains of Tillietudlem; ' it's an
unco thing that decent folk should be harled through
the country this gate, as if they were a warld's
wonder.'

' I am sorry to see you here, Cuddie,' said Morton, who, even in his own distress, did not lose
feeling for that of others.

' And sae am I, Mr Henry,' answered Cuddie,
' baith for mysel and you; but niether of our sorrows will do muckle gude that I can see. To be
sure, for me,' continued the captive agriculturist,
relieving his heart by talking, though he well knew
it was to little purpose,—' to be sure, for my part,
I hae nae right to be here ava', for I never did nor
said a word against either king or curate; but my
mother, puir body, couldna haud the auld tongue
o' her, and we maun baith pay for't, it's like.'

' Your mother is their prisoner likewise?' said
Morton, hardly knowing what he said.

' In troth is she, riding ahint ye there like a bride
wi' that auld carle o' a minister, that they ca' Gabriel Kettledrummle—De'il that he had-been in the

inside of a drum or a kettle either, for my share o'
him! Ye see, we were nae sooner chased out o' the
doors o' Milnwood, and your uncle and the housekeeper banging them to and barring them ahint us,
as if we had had the plague on our bodies, than I
says to my mother, What are we to do neist, for
every hole and bore in the country will be steekit
against us, now that ye hae affronted my auld leddy,
and gar't the troopers tak up young Milnwood? Sae
she says to me, Binna cast doun, but gird yoursel
up to the great task o' the day, and gi'e your testimony like a man upon the mount o' the Covenant.'

'And so I suppose you went to a conventicle?'
said Morton.

'Ye sall hear,' continued Cuddie.—' Aweel, I
kenn'd na muckle better what to do, sae I e'en ga'ed
wi' her to an auld daft carline like hersel, and we
gat some water-broo and bannocks; and mony a
weary grace they said, and mony a psalm they sung,
or they wad let me win to, for I was amaist famished wi' vexation. Aweel, they had me up in the
gray o' the morning and I behoved to whig awa'
wi' them, reason or nane, to a great gathering o'
their folk at the Miry-sikes, and there this chield,
Gabriel Kettledrummle, was blasting awa' to them
on the hill-side, about lifting up their testimony, nae
doubt, and ganging down to the battle of Ramoth
Gilead, or some sic a place. Eh, Mr. Henry! but
the carle gae them a screed o' doctrine! Ye might
hae heard him a mile down the wind—He' routed
like a cow in a fremd loaning.—Weel, thinks I,
there's nae place in this country they ca' Roman
Gilead—it will be some gate in the west moorlands;
and or we win there I'll see to slip awa' wi' this

mother o' mine, for I winna rin my neck into a
tether for ony Kettledrummle in the country side.
—Aweel,' continued Cuddie, relieving himself by
detailing his misfortunes, without being scrupulous
concerning the degree of attention which his companion bestowed on his narrative, ' just as I was
wearying for the tail o' the preaching, cam word
that the dragoons were upon us.—Some ran, and
some cried stand, and some cried down wi' the
Philistines—I was at my mother to get her awa'
sting and ling or the red-coats cam up, but I might
as weel hae tried to drive our auld fore-a-hand ox
without the goad—de'il a step wad she budge.—
Weel, after a', the cleugh we were in was strait,
and the mist cam thick, and there was gude hope
the dragoons wad hae missed us if we could hae
held our ain tongues; but, as if auld Kettledrummle
himsel hadna made din aneuch to waken the very
dead, they behoved a' to skirl up a psalm that ye
wad hae heard as far as Lanrick!—Aweel, to mak
a lang tale short, up cam my young Lord Evandale,
skelping as fast as his horse could trot, and twenty
red-coats at his back. Twa or three chields wad
needs fight, wi' the pistol and the whinger in the
tae hand, and the Bible in the tother, and they got
their crowns weel clowred; but there was nae muckle
skaith dune, for Evandale aye cried to scatter us,
but to spare life.'

' And did you not resist?' said Morton, who
probably felt, that, at that moment, he himself
would have encountered Lord Evandale on much
slighter grounds.

'Na truly,' answered Cuddie, ' I keepit aye be-
for the auld woman, and cried for mercy to life

and limb; but twa o' the red-coats cam up, and ane
o' them was gaun to strike my mother wi' the
side o' his broadsword—So I got up my kebbie at
them, and said I wad gi'e them as gude. Weel,
they turned on me, and clinked at me with their
swords, and I garr'd my hand keep my head as weel
as I could till Lord Evandale cam up, and then I
cried out I was a servant at Tillietudlem—ye ken
yoursel he was aye judged to hae a look after the
young leddy—and he bade me fling doun my kent,
and sae me and my mother yielded oursels prisoners.—I'm thinking we wad hae been letten slip awa',
but Kettledrummle was ta'en near us, for Andrew
Wilson's naig that he was riding on had been a
dragooner lang syne, and the sairer Kettledrummle
spurred to win awa', the readier the dour beast ran
to the dragoons when he saw them draw up.—
Aweel, when my mother and him forgathered, they
set till the sodgers, and I think they gae them their
kale through the reek! Bastards o' the whore of
Babylon was the best words in their wame. Sae
then the kiln was in a bleeze again, and they brought
us a' three on wi' them to mak us an example, as
they ca't.'

'It is most infamous and intolerable oppression,'
said Morton half speaking to himself; 'here is a
poor peaceable fellow, whose only motive for joining the conventicle was a sense of filial piety, and
he is chained up like a thief or murderer, and likely to die the death of one, but without the privilege
of a formal trial, which our law indulges to the
worst malefactor! Even to witness such tyranny,
and still more to suffer under it, is enough to make
the blood of the tamest slave boil within him.'

'To be sure,' said Cuddie, hearing and partly understanding what had broken from Morton in resentment of his injuries, ' it is no right to speak evil o' dignities—my auld leddy aye said that, as nae doubt she had a gude right to do, being in a place o' dignity hersel; and troth I listened to her very patiently, for she aye ordered a dram, or a sowp kale, or something to us, after she had gi'en us a hearing on our duties. But de'il a dram, or kale, or ony thing else—no sae muckle as a cup o' cauld water do thae lords at Edinburgh gi'e us; and yet they are heading and hanging amang us, and trailing us after thae blackguard troopers, and taking our goods and gear as if we were outlaws. I canna say I tak it kind at their hands.'

'It would be very strange if you did,' answered Morton, with suppressed emotion.

'And what I like warst o' a',' continued poor Cuddie, ' is thae ranting red-coats coming amang the lasses and taking awa our joes. I had a sair heart o' my ain when I passed the Mains down at Tillietudlem this morning about parritch-time, and saw the reek coming out at my ain lum-head, and kenn'd there was some ither body than my auld mither sitting by the ingle-side. But I think my heart was e'en sairer when I saw that hellicat trooper, Tam Halliday, kissing Jenny Dennison afore my face. I wonder women can hae the impudence to do sic things; but they are a' for the red-coats. Whiles I hae thought o' being a trooper mysel, when I thought naething else wad gae down wi' Jenny—and yet I'll no blame her ower muckle neither, for maybe it was a' for my sake that she loot Tam touzle her tap-knots that gate.'

'For your sake?' said Morton, unable to refrain from taking some interest in a story which seemed to bear a singular coincidence with his own.

'E'en sae, Milnwood,' replied Cuddie; 'for the puir quean gat leave to come near me wi' speaking the loon fair, (d—n him, that I suld say sae) and sae she bade me God speed, and she wanted to stap siller into my hand;—I'se warrant it was the tae half o' her fee and bountith, for she wared the ither half on pinners and pearlings to gang to see us shoot yon day at the popinjay.'

'And did you take it, Cuddie?' said Morton.

'Troth did I no, Milnwood; I was sic a fule as to fling it back to her—my heart was ower grit to be behadden to her, when I had seen that loon slavering and kissing at her. But I was a great fule for my pains; it wad hae dune my mother and me some gude, and she'll ware't a' on duds and nonsense.'

There was here a deep and long pause. Cuddie was probably engaged in regretting the rejection of his mistress's bounty, and Henry Morton in considering from what motives, or upon what conditions, Miss Bellenden had succeeded in procuring the interference of lord Evandale in his favour.

'Was it not possible,' suggested his awakening hopes, 'that he had construed her influence over lord Evandale hastily and unjustly? Ought he to censure her severely, if, submitting to dissimulation for his sake, she had permitted the young nobleman to entertain hopes which she had no intention to realize? Or what if she had appealed to the generosity which lord Evandale was supposed to possess,

and had engaged his honour to protect the person of
a favoured rival?'

Still, however, the words which we had overheard
recurred ever and anon to his remembrance, with a
pang which resembled the sting of an adder.

' Nothing that she could refuse him!—was it possible to make a more unlimited declaration of predilection? The language of affection has not, within
the limits of maidenly delicacy, a stronger expression. She is lost to me wholly, and for ever; and
nothing remains for me now, but vengeance for my
own wrongs, and for those which are hourly inflicted on my country.'

Apparently, Cuddie, though with less refinement,
was following out a similar train of ideas; for he
suddenly asked Morton, in a low whisper,—' Wad
there be ony ill in getting out o' thae chields' hands
an' ane could compass it?'

' None in the world,' said Morton; ' and if an opportunity occurs of doing so, depend on it I for one
will not let it slip.'

' I'm blythe to hear ye say sae,' answered Cuddie.
' I am but a puir silly fallow, but I canna think there
wad be muckle ill in breaking out by strength o'
hand, if ye could mak it ony thing feasible. I am
the lad that will ne'er fear to lay on, if it were come
to that; but our auld leddy wad hae ca'd that a resisting o' the king's authority.'

' I will resist any authority on earth,' said Morton, ' that invades tyrannically my chartered rights
as a freeman; and I am determined I will not be
unjustly dragged to a jail, or perhaps a gibbet, if I
can possibly make my escape from these men either
by address or force.'

'Weel, that's just my mind too, aye supposing we hae a feasible opportunity o' breaking loose. But then ye speak o' a charter; now these are things that only belang to the like o' you, that are a gentleman, and it might na bear me through, that am but a husbandman.'

'The charter that I speak of,' said Morton, 'is common to the meanest Scotchman. It is that freedom from stripes and bondage which was claimed, as you may read in Scripture, by the Apostle Paul himself, and which every man who is free-born is called upon to defend, for his own sake and that of his countrymen.'

'Hegh, sirs!' replied Cuddie, 'it wad hae been lang or my leddy Margaret, or my mither either, wad hae fund out sic a wiselike doctrine in the Bible! The tane was aye graning about giving tribute to Cæsar, and the tither is as daft wi' her whiggery. I hae been clean spoilt, just wi' listening to twa blethering auld wives; but if I could get a gentleman that wad let me tak on to be his servant, I am confident I wad be a clean contrary creature; and I hope your honour will think on what I am saying, if we were ance fairly delivered out o' this house of bondage, and just tak me to be your ain wally-de-shamble.'

'My valet, Cuddie?' answered Morton, 'alas! that would be sorry preferment, even if we were at liberty.'

'I ken what ye're thinking—that because I am landward bred, I wad be bringing ye to disgrace afore folk; but ye maun ken I'm gay gleg at the uptak; there was never ony thing dune wi' hand but I learned gay readily, 'septing reading, writing, and cyphering; but there's no the like o' me at the fit-ba', and I can play wi' the broadsword as weel as corporal Inglis there. I hae broken his head or now, for as massy as he's riding ahint us.——And then ye'll no be gaun to stay in this country?'——said he, stopping and interrupting himself.

' Probably not,' replied Morton.

' Weel, I care na a boddle. Ye see I wad get my mither bestowed wi' her auld graning tittie, auntie Meg, in the Gallowgate o' Glasgow, and then I trust they wad neither burn her for a witch, or let her fail for fau't o' fude, or hang her up for an auld whig wife; for the provost, they say, is very regard-ful o' sic puir bodies. And then you and I wad gang and pouss our fortunes, like the folk i' the daft auld tales about Jock the Giant-killer and Va-lentine and Orson; and we wad come back to mer-ry Scotland, as the sang says, and I wad tak to the stilts again, and turn sic furs on the bonnie rigs o' Milnwood holms, that it wad be worth a pint but to look at them.'

' I fear,' said Morton, ' there is very little chance, my good friend Cuddie, of our getting back to your old occupation.'

' Hout, sir—hout, sir,' replied Cuddie, ' it's aye gude to keep up a hardy heart—as broken a ship's come to land.—But what's that I hear?—never stir, if my auld mither is na at the preaching again! I ken the sough o' her texts, that sound just like the wind blawing through the spence; and there's Ket-tledrummle setting to wark, too—Lord's sake, if the sodgers anes get angry, they'll murder them baith, and us for company!'

Their farther conversation was in fact interrupted by a blatant noise which arose behind them, in which the voice of the preacher emitted, in unison with that of the old woman, tones like the grumble of a bassoon combined with the screaking of a cracked fiddle. At first, the aged pair of sufferers had been contented to condole with each other in smothered expressions of complaint and indignation; but the sense of their injuries became more pungently aggravated as they communicated with each other, and they became at length unable to suppress their ire.

' Woe, woe, and a threefold woe unto you, ye bloody and violent persecutors!' exclaimed the reverend Gabriel Kettledrummle—' Woe, and threefold woe unto you, even to the breaking of seals, the blowing of trumpets, and the pouring forth of vials!'

' Ay—ay—a black cast to a' their ill-fa'ar'd faces, and the outside o' the loof to them at the last day,' echoed the shrill counter-tenor of Mause, falling in like the second part of a catch.

' I tell you,' continued the divine, ' that your rankings and your ridings—your neighings and your prancings—your bloody, barbarous, and inhuman cruelties—your benuming, deadening, and debauching the consciences of poor creatures by oaths, soul-damning and self-contradictory, have risen from earth to Heaven like a foul and hideous outcry of perjury for hastening the wrath to come——hugh! hugh! hugh!'

' And I say,' cried Mause, in the same tune, and nearly at the same time, ' that wi' this auld breath o' mine, and it's sair ta'en down wi' the asthmatics and this rough trot'——

' De'il gin they would gallop,' said Cuddie, ' wad
it but gar her haud her tongue!'

' Wi' this auld and brief breath,' continued
Mause, ' will I testify against the backslidings, de-
fections, defalcations, and declinings, of the land—
against the grievances and the causes of wrath.'

' Peace, I pr'ythee—Peace, good woman,' said
the preacher, who had just recovered from a violent
fit of coughing, and found his own anathema borne
down by Mause's better wind, ' peace, and take not
the word out of the mouth of a servant of the altar.—I say, I uplift my voice and tell ye, that before the play is played out—ay, before this very sun
gaes down, ye sall learn that neither a desperate
Judas, like your prelate Sharpe that's gone to his
place; nor a sanctuary-breaking Holofernes, like
bloody-minded Claverhouse; nor an ambitious Dio-
trephes, like the lad Evandale; nor a covetous and
warld following Demas, like him they ca' serjeant
Bothwell, that makes every wife's plack and her
meal-ark his ain; neither your carabines, nor your
pistols, nor your broadswords, nor your horses, nor
your saddles, bridles, sarcingles, nose-bags, nor
martingales, shall resist the arrows that are whetted
and the bow that is bent against you.'

' That shall they never, I trow,' echoed Mause;
' castaways are they ilk ane o' them—besoms of destruction, fit only to be flung into the fire when they
have sweepit the filth out o' the Temple—whips of
small cords, knotted for the chastisement of those
wha like their warldly gudes and gear better than
the Cross or the Covenant, but when that wark's
done, only meet to mak latchets to the de'il's
brogues.'

' Fiend hae me,' said Cuddie, addressing himself
to Morton, ' if I dinna think our mither preaches
as weel as the minister!—But it's a sair pity o' his
hoast, for it aye comes on just when he's at the best
o't, and that lang routing he made air this morning
is sair again him too—De'il an I care if he wad
roar her dumb, and than he wad hae't a' to answer
for himsel—it's lucky the road's rough, and the
troopers are no taking muckle tent to what they say
wi' the rattling o' the horses feet; but an' we were
anes on saft grund, we'll hear news o' a' this.'

Cuddie's conjectures were but too true. The
words of the prisoners had not been much attended
to while drowned by the clang of the horses' hoofs
on a rough and stony road; but they now entered
upon the moorland, where the testimony of the two
zealous captives lacked this saving accompaniment.
And, accordingly, no sooner had their steeds begun
to tread heath and green sward, and Gabriel Kettledrummle had again raised his voice with, ' Also
I uplift my song like that of a pelican in the wilderness'——

' And I mine,' had issued from Mause, ' like a
sparrow on the house-tops'——

When, ' Hollo, ho!' cried the corporal from the
rear; ' rein up your tongues, the devil blister them,
or I'll clap a martingale on them.'

' I will not peace at the commands of the profane,' said Gabriel.

' Nor I neither,' said Mause, ' for the bidding of
no earthly potsherd, though it be painted as red as
a brick of the tower of Babel, and ca' itsel a corporal.'

' Halliday,' cried the corporal, ' hast got never a gag about thee, man?—We must stop their mouths before they talk us all dead.'

Ere any answer could be made, or any measure taken in consequence of the corporal's motion, a dragoon gallopped towards serjeant Bothwell, who was considerably a-head of the party he commanded. On hearing the orders which he brought, Bothwell instantly rode back to the head of his party, ordered them to close their files, to mend their pace, and to move with silence and precaution, as they would soon be in presence of the enemy.

CHAPTER XV.

Quantum in nobis, we've thought good
To save the expense of Christian blood,
And try if we, by mediation,
Of treaty, and accommodation,
Can end the quarrel, and compose
This bloody duel without blows.   *Butler.*

THE increased pace of the party of horsemen soon took away from their zealous captives the breath, if not the inclination, necessary for holding forth. They had now for more than a mile got free of the woodlands, whose broken glades had, for some time, accompanied them after they had left the woods of Tillietudlem. A few birches and oaks still feathered the narrow ravines, or occupied in dwarf clusters the hollow plains of the moor. But these were gradually disappearing; and a wide and

waste country lay before them, swelling into hills
of dark heath, intersected by deep gullies, being the
passages by which torrents forced their course in
winter, and, during summer, the disproportioned
channels for diminutive rivulets that winded their
puny way among heaps of stones and gravel, the
effects and tokens of their winter fury,—like so
many spendthrifts dwindled down by the consequences of former excesses and extravagance. This
desolate region seemed to extend farther than the
eye could reach, without grandeur, without even
the dignity of mountain wildness, yet striking, from
the huge proportion which it seemed to bear to
such more favoured spots of the country as were
adapted to cultivation and fitted for the support
of man; and thereby impressing irresistibly the
mind of the spectator with a sense of the omnipo-
tence of nature, and the comparative inefficacy of the
boasted means of amelioration which man is capable of opposing to the disadvantages of climate and
soil.

It is a remarkable effect of such extensive wastes,
that they impose an idea of solitude even upon
those who travel through them in considerable numbers; so much is the imagination affected by the
disproportion between the desert around and the
party who are traversing it. Thus the members of
a caravan of a thousand souls may feel, in the deserts of Africa or Arabia, a sense of loneliness unknown to the individual traveller, whose solitary
course is through a thriving and cultivated country.

It was not, therefore, without a peculiar feeling
of emotion, that Morton beheld, at the distance of
about half a mile, the body of cavalry to which his

escort belonged, creeping up a steep and winding path which ascended from the more level moor into the hills. Their numbers, which appeared formidable when they crowded through narrow roads, and seemed multiplied by appearing partially, and at different points, among the trees, were now apparently diminished by being exposed at once to view, and in a landscape whose extent bore such immense proportion to the column of horses and men, that, showing more like a drove of black cattle than a body of soldiers, crawled slowly along the face of the hill, their force and their numbers seeming trifling and contemptible.

' Surely,' said Morton to himself, ' a handful of resolute men may defend any defile in these mountains against such a small force as this is, providing that their bravery is equal to their enthusiasm.'

While he made these reflections, the rapid movement of the horsemen who guarded him soon traversed the space which divided them from their companions, and ere the front of Claverhouse's column had gained the brow of the hill which they had been seen ascending, Bothwell, with his rearguard and prisoners, had united himself, or nearly so, with the main body led by his commander. The extreme difficulty of the road, which was in some places steep, and in others boggy, retarded the progress of the column, especially in the rear; for the passage of the main body, in many instances, potched up the swamps through which they passed, and rendered them so deep, that the last of their followers were forced to leave the beaten path, and find safer passage where they could.

On these occasions, the distresses of the Reverend Gabriel Kettledrummle and of Mause Headrigg were considerably augmented, as the brutal troopers, by whom they were guarded, compelled them, at all risks which such inexperienced riders were likely to incur, to leap their horses over drains and gullies, or to push them through morasses and swamps.

'Through the help of the Lord I have leaped over a wall,' exclaimed poor Mause as her horse was, by her rude attendants, brought up to leap the turf inclosure of a deserted fold, in which feat her curch flew off, leaving her gray hairs uncovered.

'I am sunk in deep mire where there is no standing—I am come into deep waters where the floods overflow me,' exclaimed Kettledrummle, as the charger on which he was mounted plunged up to the saddle-girths in a *well-head*, as they call the springs which supply the marshes, the sable streams beneath spouting over the face and person of the captive preacher.

These exclamations excited shouts of laughter among their military attendants; but events soon occurred which rendered them all sufficiently serious.

The leading files of the regiment had nearly attained the brow of the steep hill we have mentioned, when two or three horsemen, speedily discovered to be a part of their own advanced guard, who had acted as patrole, appeared returning at full gallop, their horses much blown, and the men apparently in a disordered flight. They were followed upon the spur by five or six riders, well-armed with sword and pistol, who halted upon the top of the hill, on observing the approach of the Life Guards. One er two who had carabines dismounted, and, taking a leisurely and deliberate aim at the foremost rank of the regiment, discharged their pieces, by which two troopers were wounded, one severely. They then mounted their horses, and disappeared over the ridge of the hill, retreating with so much coolness as evidently showed, that, on the one hand, they were undismayed by the approach of so considerable a force as was moving against them, and conscious, on the other, that they were supported by numbers sufficient for their protection. This incident occasioned a halt through the whole body of cavalry; and while Claverhouse himself received the report of his advanced-guard, which had been thus driven back upon the main body, Lord Evandale advanced to the top of the ridge over which the enemy's horsemen had retired, and Major Allan, Cornet Grahame, and the other officers, employed themselves in extricating the regiment from the broken ground, and drawing them up upon the side of the hill in two lines, the one to support the other.

The word was then given to advance; and in a few minutes the first line stood on the brow, and commanded the prospect on the other side. The second line closed upon them, and also the rear-guard with the prisoners; so that Morton and his companions in captivity could, in like manner, see the form of opposition which was now offered to the further progress of their captors.

The brow of the hill, on which the royal Life Guards were now drawn up, sloped downwards (on the side opposite to that which they had ascended) with a gentle declivity, for more than a quarter of

a mile, and presented ground, which, though unequal in some places, was not altogether unfavourable for the manœuvres of cavalry, until nigh the
bottom, when the slope terminated in a marshy level, traversed through its whole length by what
seemed either a natural gulley, or a deep artificial
drain, the sides of which were broken by springs,
trenches filled with water, out of which peats and
turfs had been dug, and here and there by some
straggling thickets of alders, which loved the mois-
ture so well, that they continued to live as bush-
es, although too much dwarfed by the sour soil and
the stagnant bog-water to ascend into trees. Beyond
this ditch, or gulley, the ground arose into a second
heathy swell, or rather hill, near to the foot of which,
and as if with the purpose of defending the broken
ground and ditch which covered their front, the
body of insurgents appeared to be drawn up with
the purpose of abiding battle.

Their infantry was divided into three lines. The
first, tolerably provided with fire-arms, were advanced almost close to the verge of the bog, so that
their fire must necessarily annoy the royal cavalry
as they descended the opposite hill, the whole front
of which was exposed, and would probably be yet
more fatal if they attempted to cross the morass.
Behind the first line was a body of pikemen, designed for their support in case the dragoons should
force the passage of the marsh. In their rear was
the third line, consisting of countrymen armed with
scythes set straight on the poles; hay-forks, spits,
clubs, goads, fish-spears, and such other rustic im-
plements as hasty resentment had converted into
instruments of war. On each flank of the infantry,

but a little backward from the bog, as if to allow
themselves dry and sound ground whereon to act
in case their enemies should force the pass, there
was drawn up a small body of cavalry, who were,
in general, but indifferently armed, and worse mounted, but full of zeal for the cause, being chiefly either landholders of small property, or farmers of the
better class, whose means enabled them to serve on
horseback. A few of those who had been engaged
in driving back the advanced guard of the royalists,
might now be seen returning slowly towards their
own squadrons. These were the only individuals
of the insurgent army which seemed to be in motion. All the others stood firm and motionless, as
the gray stones that lay scattered on the heath
around them.

The total number of the insurgents might amount
to about a thousand men; but of these there were
scarce a hundred cavalry, nor were the one half of
them even tolerably armed. The strength of their
position, however, the sense of their having taken a
desperate step, the superiority of their numbers, but,
above all, the ardour of their enthusiasm, were the
means on which their leaders reckoned for supply-
ing the want of arms, equipage, and military discipline.

On the side of the hill which rose above the array of battle which they had adopted, were seen the
women, and even the children, whom zeal, opposed
to persecution, had driven into the wilderness. They
seemed stationed there to be spectators of the en-
gagement by which their own fate, as well as that
of their parents, husbands, and sons, was to be decided. Like the females of the ancient German

tribes, the shrill cries which they raised, when they beheld the glittering ranks of their enemy appear on the brow of the opposing eminence, acted as an incentive to their relatives to fight to the last in defence of that which was dearest to them. Such exhortations seemed to have their full and emphatic effect; for a wild halloo, which went from rank to rank on the appearance of the soldiers, intimated the resolution of the insurgents to fight to the uttermost.

As the horsemen halted their lines on the ridge of the hill, their trumpets and kettle-drums sounded a bold and warlike flourish of menace and defiance, that rang along the waste like the shrill summons of a destroying angel. The wanderers, in answer, united their voices, and sent forth, in solemn modulation the two first verses of the seventy-sixth Psalm, according to the metrical version of the Scotish Kirk:

'In Judah's land God is well known,
  His name's in Israel great,
In Salem is his tabernacle,
  In Zion is his seat.

There arrows of the bow he brake,
  The shield, the sword, the war,
More glorious thou than hills of prey,
  More excellent art far.'

A shout, or rather a solemn acclamation, attended the close of the stanza; and, after a dead pause, the second verse was resumed by the insurgents, who applied the destruction of the Assyrians as prophetical of the issue of their own impending contest:—

Those that were stout of heart, were spoil'd,
　　They slept their sleep outright,
And none of those their hands did find,
　　That were the men of might.

When thy rebuke, O Jacob's God,
　　Had forth against them past,
　Their horses and their chariots both
　　Were in a dead sleep cast.'

There was another acclamation, which was followed by the most profound silence.

While these solemn sounds, accented by a thousand voices, were prolonged amongst the waste hills, Claverhouse looked with great attention on the ground, and on the order of battle which the wanderers had adopted, and in which they determined to await the assault.

'The churles,' he said, 'must have some old soldiers with them; it was no rustic that made choice of that ground.'

'Burley is said to be with them for certain,' answered Lord Evandale, 'and also Hackstoun of Rathillet, Paton of Meadowhead, Cleland, and some other men of military skill.'

'I judged as much,' said Claverhouse, 'from the style in which these detached horsemen leapt their horses over the ditch, as they returned to their position. It was easy to see that there were a few round-headed troopers amongst them, the true spawn of the old Covenant. We must manage this matter warily as well as boldly. Evandale, let the officers come to this knoll.'

He moved to a small moss-grown cairn, probably the resting-place of some Celtic chief of other

times, and the call of, ' Officers to the front,' soon
brought them around their commander.

' I did not call you round me, gentlemen,' said
Claverhouse, ' in the formal capacity of a council
of war, for I will never turn over on others the responsibility which my rank imposes on myself.   I
only want the benefit of your opinions, reserving to
myself, as most men do when they ask advice, the
liberty of following my own.—What say you, Cornet Grahame? Shall we attack these fellows who are
bellowing yonder? You are youngest and hottest,
and therefore will speak first whether I will or no.'

' Then,' said Cornet Grahame, ' while I have
the honour to carry the standard of the Life Guards,
it shall never, with my will, retreat before rebels. I
say, charge, in God's name and the King's!'

' And what say you, Allan?' continued Claverhouse; ' for Evandale is so modest we shall never
get him to speak till you have said what you have
to say.'

' These fellows,' said Major Allan, an old cavalier officer of experience, ' are three or four to one—
I should not mind that much upon a fair field, but
they are posted in a very formidable strength, and
show no inclination to quit it.   I therefore think,
with deference to Cornet Grahame's opinion, that
we should draw back to Tillietudlem, occupy the
pass between the hills and the open country, and
send for reinforcements to my Lord Ross, who is
lying at Glasgow with a regiment of infantry.   In
this way we should cut them off from the strath of
Clyde, and either compel them to come out of their
strong-hold, and give us battle on fair terms, or, if
they remain here, we will attack them so soon as

our infantry has joined us, and enabled us to act with effect among these ditches, bogs, and quagmires.'

' Pshaw,' said the young Cornet, ' what signifies strong ground, when it is only held by a crew of canting, psalm-singing old women?'

' A man may fight never the worse,' retorted Major Allan, ' for honouring both his Bible and psalter. These fellows will prove as stubborn as steel. I know them of old.'

' Their nasal psalmody,' said the Cornet, ' reminds our major of the race of Dunbar.'

' Had you been at that race, young man,' retorted Allan, ' you would have wanted nothing to remind you of it for the longest day you had to live.'

' Hush, hush, gentlemen,' said Claverhouse, ' these are untimely repartees.—I should like your advice well, major Allan, had our rascally patroles (whom I will see duly punished) brought us timely notice of the enemy's numbers and position. But having once presented ourselves before them in line, the retreat of the life guards would argue gross timidity, and be the general signal for insurrection through the west. In which case, so far from obtaining any assistance from my Lord Ross, I promise you I should have great apprehensions of his being cut off before we could join him, or he us. A retreat would have quite the same fatal effect upon the king's cause as the loss of a battle— and as to the difference of risk or of safety it might make with respect to ourselves, that, I am sure, no gentleman thinks a moment about. There must be some gorges or passes in the morass through which we can force our way; and, were we once on firm ground, I trust there is no man in the life guards who supposes our squadrons, though so weak in numbers, are unable to trample into dust twice the number of these unpractised clowns.——What say you, my lord Evandale?'

' I humbly think,' said lord Evandale, ' that, go the day how it will, it must be a bloody one; and that we shall lose many brave fellows, and probably be obliged to slaughter a great number of these misguided men, who, after all, are Scotchmen and subjects of King Charles, as well as we are.'

' Rebels! rebels! and undeserving the name either of Scotchmen or of subjects,' said Claverhouse; ' but come, my lord, what does your opinion point at?'

' To enter into a treaty with these ignorant and misled men.'

' A treaty, and with rebels having arms in their hands? Never while I live,' answered his commander.

' At least send a trumpet and flag of truce, summoning them to lay down their weapons and disperse,' said lord Evandale, ' upon promise of a free pardon—I have always heard that had that been done before the battle of Pentland-hills, much blood might have been saved.'

' Well,' said Claverhouse, ' and who the devil do you think would carry a summons to these head-strong and desperate fanatics? They acknowledge no laws of war. Their leaders, who have been all most active in the murder of the Archbishop of St. Andrews, fight with a rope round their necks, and are likely to kill the messenger, were it but to dip their followers in loyal blood, and to make them as desperate of pardon as themselves.

'I will go myself,' said Evandale, 'if you will permit me. I have often risked my blood to spill that of others, let me now do so in order to save human lives.'

'You shall not go on such an errand, my lord,' said Claverhouse; 'your rank and situation render your safety of too much consequence to the country in an age when good principles are so rare!—Here's my brother's son, Dick Grahame, who fears shot or steel as little as if the devil had given him armour of proof against it, as the fanatics say he has given to his uncle. He shall take a flag-of-truce and a trumpet, and ride down to the edge of the morass to summon them to lay down their arms and disperse.'

'With all my soul, colonel,' answered the cornet; 'and I'll tie my cravat on a pike to serve for a white flag—the rascals never saw such a pennon of Flanders lace in their lives before.'

'Colonel Grahame,' said Evandale, while the young officer prepared for his expedition, 'this young gentleman is your nephew and your apparent heir; for God's sake, permit me to go. It was my counsel, and I ought to stand the risk.'

'Were he my only son,' said Claverhouse, 'this is no cause and no time to spare him. I hope my private affections will never interfere with my public duty. If Dick Grahame falls, the loss is chiefly mine; were your lordship to die, the king and country would be the sufferers.—Come, gentlemen, each to his post. If our summons is unfavourably received, we will instantly attack, and, as the old Scotish blazon has it, God save the right!'

CHAPTER XVI.

With many a stout thwack and many a bang,
Hard crab-tree and old iron rang.　　　*Hudibras.*

CORNET RICHARD GRAHAME descended the hill, bearing in his hand the extempore flag of truce, and making his managed horse keep time by bounds and curvets to the tune which he whistled. The trumpeter followed. Five or six horsemen, having something the appearance of officers, detached themselves from each flank of the presbyterian army, and, meeting in the centre, approached the ditch which divided the hollow as near as the morass would permit. Towards this group, but keeping the opposite side of the swamp, Cornet Grahame directed his horse, his motions being now the conspicuous object of attention to both armies; and, without disparagement to the courage of either, it is probable there was a general wish on both sides that this embassy might save the risks and bloodshed of the impending conflict.

When he had arrived right opposite to those, who, by their advancing to receive his message, seemed to take upon themselves as the leaders of the enemy, Cornet Crahame commanded his trumpeter to sound a parley. The insurgents having no instrument of martial music wherewith to make the appropriate reply, one of their number called out with a loud, strong voice, demanding to know why he approached their leaguer.

' To summon you in the king's name, and in that of colonel John Grahame of Claverhouse, specially

commissioned by the right honourable privy council of Scotland,' answered the cornet, ' to lay down
your arms and dismiss the followers whom ye have
led into rebellion, contrary to the laws of God, of
the king, and of the country.'

' Return to them that sent thee,' said the insurgent leader, ' and tell them that we are this day in
arms for a broken covenant and a persecuted kirk;
tell them that we renounce the licentious and perjured Charles Stuart, whom you call king, even as
he renounced the covenant, after having once and
again sworn to prosecute to the utmost of his power
all the ends thereof, really, constantly, and sincerely,
all the days of his life, having no enemies but the
enemies of the covenant, and no friends but its
friends. Whereas, far from keeping the oath he
had called God and angels to witness, his first step,
after his incoming into these kingdoms, was the
fearful grasping at the prerogative of the Almighty,
by that hideous act of Supremacy, together with
his expulsing, without summons, libel, or process
of law, hundreds of famous faithful preachers, thereby wringing the bread of life out of the mouth of
hungry, poor creatures, and forcibly cramming their
throats with the lifeless, saltless, foisonless, luke-
warm drammock of the fourteen false prelates, and
their sycophantic, formal, carnal, scandalous crea-
ture-curates.'

' I did not come to hear you preach,' answered
the officer, ' but to know in one word, if you will
disperse yourselves, on condition of a free pardon
to all but the murderers of the late archbishop of
St. Andrews; or whether you will abide the attack

of his majesty's forces, which will instantly advance upon you.'

'In one word, then,' answered the spokesman, 'we are here with our swords on our thighs, as men that watch in the night. We will take one part and portion together, as brethren in righteousness. Whosoever assails us in our good cause, his blood be on his own head. So return to them that sent thee, and God give them and thee a sight of the evil of your ways!'

'Is not your name,' said the cornet, who began to recollect having seen the person whom he was now speaking with, 'John Balfour of Burley?'

'And if it be,' said the spokesman, 'hast thou aught to say against it?'

'Only,' said the Cornet, 'that as you are excluded from pardon in the name of the king and of my commanding officer, it is to these country people, and not to you, that I offer it; and it is not with you, or such as you, that I am sent to treat.'

'Thou art a young soldier, friend,' said Burley, 'and scant well-learned in thy trade, or thou wouldst know that the bearer of a flag of truce cannot treat with the army but through their officers; and that if he presume to do otherwise, he forfeits his safe-conduct.'

While speaking these words, Burley unslung his carabine, and held it in readiness.

'I am not to be intimidated from the discharge of my duty by the menaces of a murderer,' said cornet Grahame.—'Hear me, good people; I proclaim, in the name of the king and of my commanding officer, full and free pardon to all, excepting'——

' I give thee fair warning,' said Burley, presenting his piece.

' A free pardon to all,' continued the young officer, still addressing the body of the insurgents—
' to all but'——

' Then the Lord grant grace to thy soul—amen,'
said Burley.

With these words he fired, and cornet Richard
Grahame dropped from his horse. The shot was
mortal. The unfortunate young gentleman had only
strength to turn himself on the ground and mutter
forth, ' My poor mother!' when life forsook him in
the effort. His startled horse fled back to the regiment at the gallop, as did his scarce less-affrighted
attendant.

' What have you done?' said one of Balfour's brother officers.

' My duty,' said Balfour firmly. ' Is it not written, thou shalt be zealous even to slaying? Let
those, who dare, now venture to speak of truce or
pardon!'

Claverhouse saw his nephew fall. He turned his
eye on Evandale, while a transitory glance of inde-
scribable emotion disturbed, for a second's space,
the serenity of his features, and briefly said, ' You
see the event.'

' I will avenge him or die!' exclaimed Evandale;
and, putting his horse into motion, rode furiously
down the hill, followed by his own troop, and that of
the deceased Cornet, which broke down without orders, and each striving to be the foremost to revenge
their young officer, their ranks soon fell into confusion. These forces formed the first line of the royalists. It was in vain that Claverhouse exclaimed,

'Halt, halt! this rashness will undo us.' It was all
that he could accomplish by gallopping along the
second line, entreating, commanding, and even me-
nacing the men with his sword, that he could restrain them from following an example so conta-
gious.

'Allan,' he said, as soon as he had rendered the
men in some degree more steady, 'lead them slowly
down the hill to support Lord Evandale, who is
about to need it very much.—Bothwell, thou art a
cool and a daring fellow'——

'Ay,' muttered Bothwell, 'you can remember
that in a moment like this.'

'Lead ten file up the hollow to the right,' continued his commanding officer, 'and try every
means to get through the bog; then form and charge
the rebels in flank and rear, while they are engaged
with us in front.'

Bothwell made a signal of intelligence and obe-
dience, and moved off with his party at a rapid pace.

Mean time, the disaster which Claverhouse had
apprehended did not fail to take place. The troopers, who, with Lord Evandale, had rushed down
upon the enemy, soon found their disorderly career
interrupted by the impracticable character of the
ground. Some stuck fast in the morass as they attempted to struggle through, some recoiled from
the attempt and remained on the brink, others dispersed to seek a more favourable place to pass the
swamp. In the midst of this confusion, the first line
of the enemy, of which the foremost rank knelt, the
second stooped, and the third stood upright, poured
in a close and destructive fire that emptied at least
a score of saddles, and increased tenfold the disor-

der into which the horsemen had fallen. Lord
Evandale, in the mean time, at the head of a very
few well-mounted men, had been able to clear the
ditch, but was no sooner across than he was charged
by the left body of the enemy's cavalry, who, encouraged by the small number of opponents that had
made their way through the broken ground, set
upon them with the utmost fury, crying, ' Woe, woe
to the uncircumcised Philistines! down with Dagon
and all his adherents!'

The young nobleman fought like a lion; but most
of his followers were killed, and he himself could
not have escaped the same fate but for a heavy fire
of carabines, which Claverhouse, who had now advanced with the second line near to the ditch, poured so effectually upon the enemy, that both horse
and foot for a moment began to shrink, and Lord
Evandale, disengaged from his unequal combat, and
finding himself nearly alone, took the opportunity to
effect his retreat through the moss. But notwithstanding the loss they had sustained by Claverhouse's first fire, the insurgents became soon aware
that the advantage of numbers and of position were
so decidedly theirs, that, if they could but persist
in making a brief but resolute defence, the Life
Guards must necessarily be defeated. Their leaders
flew through their ranks, exhorting them to stand
firm, and pointing out how efficacious their fire must
be where both men and horse were exposed to it;
for the troopers, according to custom, fired without
having dismounted. Claverhouse, more than once,
when he perceived his best men dropping by a fire
which they could not effectually return, made desperate efforts to pass the bog at various points, and

renew the battle on firm ground and fiercer terms.
But the close fire of the insurgents, joined to the
natural difficulties of the pass, disappointed his at-
tempts in every point.

'We must retreat,' he said to Evandale, 'unless
Bothwell can effect a diversion in our favour. In the
mean time, draw the men out of fire, and leave skir-
mishers behind these patches of alderbushes to keep
the enemy in check.'

These directions being accomplished, the appearance of Bothwell with his party was earnestly expected. But Bothwell had his own disadvantages
to struggle with. His detour to the right had not
escaped the penetrating observation of Burley, who
made a corresponding movement with the left wing
of the mounted insurgents, so that when Bothwell,
after riding a considerable way up the valley, found
a place at which the bog could be passed, though
with some difficulty, he perceived he was still in
front of a superior enemy. His daring character
was in no degree checked by this unexpected opposition.

'Follow me, my lads,' he called to his men; never
let it be said that we turned our backs before these
canting roundheads!

With that, as if inspired by the spirit of his ances-
tors, he shouted, 'Bothwell! Bothwell!' and throwing himself into the morass, he struggled through it
at the head of his party, and attacked that of Burley with such fury, that he drove them back above
a pistol-shot, killing three men with his own hand.
Burley, perceiving the consequences of a defeat on
this point, and that his men, though more numerous,
were unequal to the regulars in using their arms

and managing their horses, threw himself across
Bothwell's way, and attacked him hand to hand.
Each of the combatants was considered as the champion of his respective party, and a result ensued
more usual in romance than in real story. Their
followers, on either side, instantly paused, and looked on as if the fate of the day were to be decided
by the event of the combat between these two re-
doubted swordsmen. The combatants themselves
seemed of the same opinion; for, after two or three
eager cuts, and pushes had been exchanged, they
paused, as if by joint consent, to recover the breath
which preceding exertions had exhausted, and to
prepare for a duel in which each seemed conscious
he had met his match.

' You are the murdering villain, Burley,' said
Bothwell, griping his sword firmly, and setting his
teeth close—' you escaped me once, but'—(he swore
an oath too tremendous to be written down) ' thy
head is worth its weight of silver, and it shall go
home at my saddle-bow, or my saddle shall go home
empty for me.'

' Yes,' replied Burley, with stern and gloomy de-
liberation, ' I am that John Balfour who promised
to lay thy head where thou should'st never lift it
again; and God do so to me, and more also, if I do
not redeem my word.'

' Then a bed of heather, or a thousand marks!'
said Bothwell, striking at Burley with his full force.

' The sword of the Lord and of Gideon!' answered
Balfour, as he parried and returned the blow.

There have seldom met two combatants more
equally matched in strength of body, skill in the
management of their weapons and horses, deter-

mined courage, and unrelenting hostility. After exchanging many desperate blows, each receiving and inflicting several wounds, though of no great consequence, they grappled together as if with the desperate impatience of mortal hate, and Bothwell, seizing his enemy by the shoulder-belt, while the grasp of Balfour was upon his own collar, they came headlong to the ground. The companions of Burley hastened to his assistance, but were repelled by the dragoons, and the battle became again general. But nothing could withdraw the attention of the combatants from each other, or induce them to unclose the deadly clasp in which they rolled together on the ground, tearing, struggling, and foaming, with the inveteracy of thorough-bred bull-dogs.

Several horses passed over them in the melée without their quitting hold of each other, until the sword-arm of Bothwell was broken by the kick of a charger. He then relinquished his grasp with a deep and suppressed groan, and both combatants started to their feet. Bothwell's right hand dropped helpless by his side, but his left griped to the place where his dagger hung; it had escaped from the sheath in the struggle,—and, with a look of mingled rage and despair, he stood totally defenceless, as Balfour, with a laugh of savage joy, flourished his sword aloft, and then passed it through his adversary's body. Bothwell received the thrust without falling—it had only grazed on his ribs. He attempted no farther defence, but, looking at Burley with a grin of deadly hatred, exclaimed,—' Base peasant churl, thou hast spilt the blood of a line of kings!'

' Die, wretch!—die,' said Balfour, redoubling the thrust with better aim; and, setting his foot on Bothwell's body as he fell, he a third time transfixed him with his sword.—' Die, blood-thirsty dog! die, as thou hast lived!—die, like the beasts that perish—hoping nothing—believing nothing.—'

' And FEARING nothing!' said Bothwell, collecting the last effort of respiration to utter these desperate words, and expiring as soon as they were spoken.

To catch a stray horse by the bridle, throw himself upon it, and rush to the assistance of his followers, was, with Burley, the affair of a moment. And as the fall of Bothwell had given to the insurgents all the courage of which it had deprived his comrades, the issue of this partial contest did not remain a moment undecided. Several soldiers were slain, the rest driven back over the morass and dispersed, and the victorious Burley, with his party, crossed it in their turn, to direct against Claverhouse the very manœuvre which he had instructed Bothwell to execute. He now put his troop in order, with the view of attacking the right wing of the royalists; and, sending news of his success to the main body, exhorted them, in the name of Heaven, to cross the marsh, and work out the glorious work of the Lord by a general attack upon the enemy.

Meanwhile, Claverhouse, who had in some degree remedied the confusion occasioned by the first irregular and unsuccessful attacl and reduced the combat in front to a distant skirmish with fire-arms, chiefly maintained by some dismounted troopers whom he had posted behind the cover of the shrubby copses of alders which, in some places, covered the edge of the morass, and whose close, cool, and well-aimed fire greatly annoyed the enemy, and concealed their own deficiency of numbers,—Cla-

verhouse, while he maintained the contest in this
manner, still expecting that a diversion by Bothwell
and his party might facilitate a general attack, was
accosted by one of the dragoons, whose bloody face
and jaded horse bore witness he was come from
hard service.

' What is the matter, Halliday?' said Claverhouse,
for he knew every man in his regiment by name—
' Where is Bothwell?'

' Bothwell is down,' replied Halliday, ' and many
a pretty fellow with him.'

' Then the king,' said Claverhouse, with his usual
composure, ' has lost a stout soldier.   The enemy
have pássed the marsh, I suppose?'

' With a strong body of horse, commanded by
the devil incarnate that killed Bothwell,' answered
the terrified soldier.

' Hush! hush!' said Claverhouse, putting his finger
on his lips ' not a word to any one but me.—Lord
Evandale, we must retreat.   The fates will have it
so. Draw together the men that are dispersed in the
skirmishing work.   Let Allan form the regiment,
and do you two retreat up the hill in two bodies,
each halting alternately as the other falls back. I'll
keep the rogues in check with the rear-guard, making a stand and facing from time to time. They will
be over the ditch presently, for I see their whole
line in motion, and preparing to cross; therefore lose
no time.'

' Where is Bothwell with his party?' said Lord
Evandale, astonished at the coolness of his commander.

' Fairly disposed of,' said Claverhouse, in his ear
—' the king has lost a servant, and the devil has

got one. But away to business, Evandale—ply your spurs and get the men together. Allan and you must keep them steady. This retreating is new work for us all; but our turn will come round again another day.'

Evandale and Allan betook themselves to their task; but ere they had arranged the regiment for the purpose of retreating in two alternate bodies, a considerable number of the enemy had crossed the marsh. Claverhouse, who had retained immediately around his person a few of his most active and tried men, charged those who had crossed in person, while they were yet disordered by the broken ground. Some they killed, others they repulsed into the morass, and checked the whole so as to enable the main body, now greatly diminished, as well as disheartened by the loss they had sustained, to commence their retreat up the hill.

But the enemy's van being soon reinforced and supported, compelled Claverhouse to follow his troops. Never did man, however, better support the character of a soldier than he did that day. Conspicuous by his black horse and white feather, he was first in the repeated charges which he made at every favourable opportunity, to arrest the progress of the pursuers, and to cover the retreat of his regiment. The object of aim to every one, he seemed as if he were impassive to their shot. The superstitious fanatics, who looked upon him as a man gifted by the Evil Spirit with supernatural means of defence, averred that they saw the bullets recoil from his jack-boots and buff coat like hailstones from a rock of granite, as he gallopped to and fro amid the storm of the battle. Many a whig that day loaded

his musket with a dollar cut into slugs, in order that
a silver bullet (such was their belief) might bring
down the persecutor of the holy kirk, on whom lead
had no power.

'Try him with the cold steel,' was the cry at
every renewed charge—'powder is wasted on him.
Ye might as weel shoot at the Auld Enemy himsel.'

But though this was loudly shouted, yet the awe
on the insurgents' mind was such, that they gave
way before Claverhouse as before a supernatural
being, and few men ventured to cross swords with
him. Still, however, he was fighting in retreat, and
with all the disadvantages attending that movement.
The soldiers behind him, as they beheld the increasing number of enemies who poured over the morass,
became unsteady; and, at every successive movement, Major Allan and Lord Evandale found it
more and more impossible to bring them to halt and
form line regularly, while, on the other hand, their
motion in the act of retreating became, by degrees,
much more rapid than was consistent with good
order. As they approached nearer to the top of the
ridge, from which in so luckless an hour they had
descended, the panic began to increase. Every one
became impatient to place the brow of the hill between him and the continued fire of the pursuers,
nor could any individual think it reasonable that he
should be the last in the retreat, and thus sacrifice
his own safety for that of others. In this mood, several troopers set spurs to their horses and fled outright, and the others became so unsteady in their
movements and formations, that their officers every
moment feared they would follow the same example.

Amid this scene of blood and confusion, the trampling of the horses, the groans of the wounded, the continued fire of the enemy, which fell in a succession of unintermitted musketry, while loud shouts accompanied each bullet which the fall of a trooper showed to have been successfully aimed—amid all the terrors and disorder of such a scene, and when it was dubious how soon they might be totally deserted by their dispirited soldiery, Evandale could not forbear remarking the composure of his commanding officer. Not at Lady Margaret's breakfast-table that morning did his eye appear more lively, or his demeanour more composed. He had closed up to Evandale for the purpose of giving some orders, and picking out a few men to reinforce his rear-guard.

‘ If this bout lasts five minutes longer,’ he said, in a whisper, ‘ our rogues will leave you, old Allan, and me, the honour of fighting this battle with our own hands. I must do something to disperse the musketeers who annoy them so hard, or we will be all shamed. Don't attempt to succour me if you see me go down, but keep at the head of your men; get off as you can, in God's name, and tell the king and the council I died in my duty.’

So saying, and commanding about twenty stout men to follow him, he gave, with this small body, a charge so desperate and unexpected, that he drove the foremost of the pursuers back to some distance. In the confusion of the assault he singled out Burley, and, desirous to strike terror into his followers, he dealt him so severe a blow on the head, as cut through his steel head-piece, and threw him from his horse, stunned for the moment, though unwounded. A wonderful thing it was afterwards thought, that one so powerful as Balfour should have sunk under the blow of a man, to appearance so slightly made as Claverhouse; and the vulgar, of course, set down to supernatural aid, the effect of that energy which a determined spirit can give to a feebler arm. Claverhouse had, in this last charge, however, involved himself too deeply among the insurgents, and was fairly surrounded.

Lord Evandale saw the danger of his commander, his body of dragoons being then halted, while that commanded by Allan was in the act of retreating. Regardless of Claverhouse's disinterested command to the contrary, he ordered the party which he headed to charge down hill and extricate their colonel. Some advanced with him—most halted and stood uncertain—many run away. With those who followed Evandale, he disengaged Claverhouse. His assistance came just in time, for a rustic had wounded his horse in a most ghastly manner by the blow of a scythe, and was about to repeat the stroke when lord Evandale cut him down. As they got out of the press, they looked round them. Allan's division had ridden clear over the hill, that officer's authority having proved altogether unequal to halt them. Evandale's divison was scattered and in total confusion.

‘ What is to be done, colonel?’ said lord Evandale.

‘ We are the last men in the field, I think,’ said Claverhouse; ‘ and when men fight as long as they can there is no shame in flying. Hector himself would say, devil take the hindmost, when there are but twenty against a thousand.—Save yourselves, my lads, and rally as soon as you can.——Come, my lord, we must e'en ride for it.'

So saying, he put spurs to his wounded horse; and the generous animal, as if conscious that the life of his rider depended on his exertions, pressed forward with speed, unabated either by pain or loss of blood. A few officers and soldiers followed him, but in a very irregular and tumultuary manner. The flight of Claverhouse was the signal for all the stragglers, who yet offered desultory resistance, to fly as fast as they could, and yield up the field of battle to the victorious insurgents.

CHAPTER XVII.

But see! through the fast-flashing lightnings of war,
What steed to the desert flies frantic and far!

Campbell.

DURING the severe skirmish of which we have given the details, Morton, together with Cuddie and his mother, and the Reverend Gabriel Kettle-drummle, remained on the brow of the hill, near to the small cairn, or barrow, beside which Claverhouse had held his preliminary council-of-war, so that they had a commanding view of the action which took place in the bottom. They were guarded by corporal Inglis and four soldiers, who, as may readily be supposed, were much more intent on watching the fluctuating fortunes of the battle, than in attending to what passed among their prisoners.

' If yon lads stand to their tackle,' said Cuddie,
' we'll hae some chance o' getting our necks out o'
the brecham again; but I misdoubt them—they hae
little skill o' arms.'

' Much is not necessary, Cuddie,' answered Morton; ' they have a strong position, and weapons in
their hands, and are more than three times the number of their assailants. If they cannot fight for their
freedom now, they and theirs deserve to lose it for-
ever.'

' O, sirs,' exclaimed Mause, here's a goodly spec-
tacle indeed! My spirit is like that of the blessed
Elihu, it burns within me—my bowels are as wine
which lacketh vent—they are ready to burst like
new bottles. O, that He may look after His ain
people in this day of judgment and deliverance!—
And now, what ailest thou, precious Mr. Gabriel
Kettledrummle? I say, what ailest thou, that wert
a Nazarite purer than snow, whiter than milk, more
ruddy than sulphur, (meaning, perhaps, sapphires)
—I say, what ails thee now, that thou art blacker
than a coal, that thy beauty is departed, and thy
loveliness withered like a dry potsherd? Surely it
is time to be up and be doing, to cry loudly and to
spare nought, and to wrestle for the puir lads that
are yonder testifying with their ain blude and that
of their enemies.'

This expostulation implied a reproach on Mr.
Kettledrummle, who, though an absolute Boanerges,
or son of thunder, in the pulpit, when the enemy
were afar, and indeed sufficiently contumacious, as
as we have seen, when in their power, had been
struck dumb by the firing, shouts, and shrieks which
now arose from the valley, and,—as many an honest

man might have been, in a situation where he could neither fight nor fly,—was too much dismayed to take so favourable an opportunity to preach the terrors of presbytery, as the courageous Mause had expected at his hand, or even to pray for the successful event of the battle. His presence of mind was not, however, entirely lost, any more than his jealous respect for his reputation as a pure and powerful preacher of the word.

' Hold your peace, woman,' he said, ' and do not perturb my inward meditations and the wrestlings wherewith I wrestle—but of a verity the shooting of the foemen doth begin to increase; peradventure, some pellet may attain unto us even here. Lo! I will ensconce me behind the cairn, as behind a strong wall or defence.'

' He's but a coward body after a',' said Cuddie, who was himself by no means deficient in that sort of courage which consists in insensibility to danger; ' he's but a daidling coward body. He'll never fill Rumbleberry's bonnet.—Odd! Rumbleberry fought and flyted like a fleeing drayon. It was a great pity, poor man, he could na cheat the woodie. But they say he gaed singing and rejoicing till't, just as I wad gang till a bicker o' brose, supposing me hungry, as I stand a gude chance to be.—Eh, sirs! yon's an awfu' sight, and yet ane canna keep their een aff frae it!'

Accordingly, strong curiosity on the part of Morton and Cuddie, together with the heated enthusiasm of old Mause, detained them on the spot from which they could best hear and see the issue of the action, leaving to Kettledrummle to occupy alone his place of security. The vicissitudes of combat, which we have already described, were witnessed by our spectators from the top of the eminence, but without their being able positively to determine to what they tended. That the presbyterians defended themselves stoutly was evident from the heavy smoke, which illuminated by frequent flashes of fire, now eddied along the valley, and hid the contending parties in its sulphurous shade. On the other hand, the continued firing from the nearer side of the morass indicated that the enemy persevered in their attack, that the affair was fiercely disputed, and that every thing was to be apprehended from a continued contest in which undisciplined rustics had to repel the assaults of regular troops so completely officered and armed.

At length horses, whose caparisons showed that they belonged to the Life-Guards, began to fly masterless out of the confusion. Dismounted soldiers next appeared, forsaking the conflict, and straggling over the side of the hill, in order to escape from the scene of action. As the numbers of these fugitives increased, the fate of the day seemed no longer doubtful. A large body was then seen emerging from the smoke, forming irregularly on the hill side, and with difficulty kept stationary by their officers, until Evandale's corps also appeared in full retreat. The result of the conflict was then apparent, and the joy of the prisoners was corrresponding to their approaching deliverance.

'They hae dune the job for anes,' said Cuddie, 'an' they ne'er do it again.'

'They flee!—they flee!' exclaimed Mause in ecstacy. 'O, the truculent tyrants! they are riding now as they never rode before. O, the false Egyptians—the proud Assyrians—the Philistines—the Moabites—the Edomites—the Ishmaelites—The Lord has brought sharp swords upon them, to make them food for the fowls of heaven and the beasts of the field. See how the clouds roll, and the fire flashes ahint them, and goes forth before the chosen of the Covenant, e'en like the pillar o' cloud and the pillar o' flame that led the people of Israel out o' the land of Egypt! This is indeed a day of deliverance to the righteous, a day of pouring out of wrath to the persecutors and the ungodly.'

'Lord safe us, mother,' said Cuddie, 'haud the clavering tongue o' ye, and lie down ahint the cairn, like Kettledrummle, honest man. Thae whigamore bullets ken unco little discretion, and will just as sune knock out the harns o' a psalm-singing auld wife as a swearing dragoon.'

'Fear naething for me, Cuddie,' said the old dame, transported to ecstacy by the success of her party; 'fear naething for me. I will stand, like Deborah, on the tap o' the cairn, and tak up my sang o' reproach against these men of Horoshteth of the Gentiles, whose horse-hoofs are broken by their prancings.'

The enthusiastic old woman would in fact have accomplished her purpose, of mounting on the cairn, and becoming, as she said, a sign and a banner to the people, had not Cuddie, with more filial tenderness than respect, detained her by such force as his shackled arms would permit him to exert.

'Eh, sirs!' he said, having accomplished this task, 'look out yonder, Milnwood; saw ye ever mortal fight like the devil Claver'se?—Yonder he's been thrice doun amang them, and thrice cam free aff.—

But I think we'll soon be free oursels, Milnwood.
Inglis and his troopers look ower their shouthers
very aften, as if they liked the road ahint them better than the road afore.'

Cuddie was not mistaken; for, when the main
tide of fugitives passed at a little distance from the
spot where they were stationed, the corporal and
his party fired their carabines at random upon the
advancing insurgents, and, abandoning all charge of
their prisoners, joined the retreat of their comrades.
Morton and the old woman, whose hands were at
liberty, lost no time in undoing the bonds of Cuddie
and of the clergyman, both of whom had been secured by a cord tied round their arms above the el-
bows. By the time this was accomplished, the rear-
guard of the dragoons, which still preserved some
order, passed beneath the hillock or rising ground
which was surmounted by the cairn already repeatedly mentioned. They exhibited all the hurry and
confusion incident to a forced retreat, but still continued in a body. Claverhouse led the van, his naked sword deeply dyed with blood, as were his face
and clothes. His horse was all covered with gore,
and now reeled with weakness. Lord Evandale,
in not much better plight, brought up the rear, still
exhorting the soldiers to keep together and fear nothing. Several of the men were wounded, and one
or two dropped from their horses as they surmounted the hill.

Mause's zeal broke forth once more at this spec-
tacle, while she stood on the heath with her head
uncovered, and her gray hairs streaming in the wind,
no bad representation of a superannuated bacchante,
or Thessalian witch in the agonies of incantation.

She soon dicovered Claverhouse at the head of his fugitive party, and exclaimed with bitter irony, ' Tarry, tarry, ye wha were aye sae blythe to be at the meetings of the saints, and wad ride every muir in Scotland to find a conventicle. Wilt thou not tarry, now thou hast found ane? Wilt thou not stay for one word mair? Wilt thou na bide the afternoon preaching?—Wae betide ye!' she said, suddenly changing her tone, ' and cut the houghs of the creature whase fleetness ye trust in!—Sheugh —Sheugh—awa' wi' ye that hae spilled sae muckle blude, and now wad save your ain—awa' wi' ye for a railing Rabshekah, a cursing Shemei, a blood-thirsty Doeg—the sword's drawn now that winna be lang o' overtaking ye, ride as fast as ye will.'

Claverhouse, it may be easily supposed, was too busy to attend to her reproaches, but hastened over the hill, anxious to get the remnant of his men out of gun-shot, in hopes of again collecting the fugitives round his standard. But as the rear of his followers rode over the ridge, a shot struck Lord Evandale's horse, which instantly sunk down dead beneath him. Two of the whig horsemen, who were the foremost in the pursuit, hastened up with the purpose of killing him, for hitherto there had been no quarter given. Morton, on the other hand, rushed forward to save his life, if possible, in order at once to indulge his natural generosity, and to requite the obligation which Lord Evandale had conferred on him that morning, and under which circumstances had made him wince so acutely. Just as he had assisted Evandale, who was much wounded, to extricate himself from his dying horse, and to gain his feet, the two horsemen came up, and one of them exclaiming, ' Have at the red-coated tyrant!' made a blow at the young nobleman, which Morton parried with difficulty, exclaiming to the rider, who was no other than Burley himself, ' Give quarter to this gentleman, for my sake—for the sake,' he added, observing that Burley did not immediately recognize him, ' of Henry Morton, who so lately sheltered you.'

' Henry Morton?' replied Burley, wiping his bloody brow with his bloodier hand, ' did I not say that the son of Silas Morton would come forth out of the land of bondage, nor be long an indweller in the tents of Ham?   Thou art a brand snatched out of the burning—But for this booted apostle of prelacy, he shall die the death!—We must smite them hip and thigh, even from the rising to the going down of the sun. It is our commission to slay them like Amalek, and utterly destroy all they have, and spare neither man nor woman, infant nor suckling; therefore hinder me not,' he continued, endeavouring again to cut down Lord Evandale, ' for this work must not be wrought negligently.'

' You must not, and you shall not slay him, more especially while incapable of defence,' said Morton, planting himself before Lord Evandale so as to intercept any blow that should be aimed at him; ' I owed my life to him this morning—my life, which was endangered solely by my having sheltered you; and to shed his blood when he can offer no effectual resistance, were not only a cruelty abhorrent to God and man, but detestable ingratitude both to him and to me.'

Burley paused—' Thou art yet,' he said, ' in the court of the Gentiles, and I compassionate thy hu-

man blindness and frailty. Strong meat is not fit
for babes, nor the mighty and grinding dispensation
under which I draw my sword, for those whose
hearts are yet dwelling in huts of clay, whose foot-
steps are tangled in the mesh of mortal sympathies,
and who clothe themselves in the righteousness
that is as filthy rags. But to gain a soul to the truth
is better than to send one to Tophet; therefore I
give quarter to this youth, providing the grant is
confirmed by the general council of God's army,
whom he hath this day blessed with so signal a deliverance.—Thou art unarmed—Abide my return
here. I must yet pursue these sinners, the Amale-
kites, and destroy then till they be utterly consumed from the face of the land, even from Havilah
unto Shur.'

So saying, he set spurs to his horse, and continued to pursue the chase.

'Cuddie,' said Morton, 'for God's sake catch a
horse as quickly as you can. I will not trust Lord
Evandale's life with these obdurate men.—You are
wounded, my Lord. Are you able to continue
your retreat?' he continued, addressing himself to
his prisoner, who, half stunned by the fall, was but
beginning to recover himself.

'I think so,' replied Lord Evandale. 'But is it
possible?—Do I owe my life to Mr. Morton?'

My interference would have been the same from
common humanity,' replied Morton; 'to your Lordship it was a sacred debt of gratitude.'

Cuddie at this instant returned with a horse.

'God-sake, mount—mount, and ride like a fleet-
ing hawk, my Lord,' said the good-natured fellow,

' for ne'er be in me, if they are na killing every ane
o' the wounded and prisoners.'

Lord Evandale mounted the horse, while Cuddie
officiously held the stirrup.

'Stand off, good fellow, thy courtesy may cost
thy life.—Mr. Morton,' he continued, addressing
Henry, ' this makes us more than even—rely on it
I will never forget your generosity—Farewell.'

He turned his horse, and rode swiftly away, in
the direction which seemed least exposed to pursuit.

Lord Evandale had just rode off, when several of
the insurgents, who were in the front of the pursuit,
came up, denouncing vengeance on Henry Morton
and Cuddie for having aided the escape of a Phil-
istine, as they called the young nobleman.

' What wad ye hae had us do?' cried Cuddie.
' Had we aught to stop a man wi', that had twa
pistols and a sword? sudna ye hae come faster up
yoursels, instead of flyting at huz?'

This excuse would hardly have passed current;
but Kettledrummle, who now awoke from his trance
of terror, and was known to, and reverenced by,
most of the wanderers, together with Mause, who
possessed their appropriate language, as well as the
preacher himself, proved active and effectual inter-
cessors.

' Touch them not, harm them not,' exclaimed
Kettledrummle, in his very best double-bass tones;
' this is the son of the famous Silas Morton, by
whom the Lord wrought great things in this land at
the breaking forth of the reformation from prelacy,
when there was a plentiful pouring forth of the
Word and a renewing of the Covenant; a hero and

champion of these blessed days, when there was power, and efficacy, and convicting, and converting of sinners, and heart-exercises, and fellowship of saints, and a plentiful flowing forth of the spices of the garden of Eden.'

' And this is my son, Cuddie,' exclaimed Mause in her turn, ' the son of his father, Juden Headrigg, wha was a douce honest man, and of me Mause Middlemas, an unworthy professor and follower of the pure gospel, and ane o' your ain folk. Is it not written, " Cut ye not off the tribes of the families of the Kothathites from among the Levites?" Numbers, fourth and seventh—O, sirs! dinna be standing here prattling wi' honest folk, when ye sud be following forth your victory with which Providence has blessed ye.'

This party having passed on, they were immediately beset by another, to whom it was necessary to give the same explanation. Kettledrummle, whose fear was much dissipated since the firing had ceased, again took upon him to be intercessor, and, grown bold, as he felt his good word necessary for the protection of his late fellow-captives, he laid claim to no small share of the merit of the victory, appealing to Morton and Cuddie, whether the tide of battle had not turned while he prayed on the Mount of Jehovah Nisi, like Moses, that Israel might prevail over Amelek; but granting them, at the same time, the credit of holding up his hands when they waxed heavy, as those of the prophet were supported by Aaron and Hur. It seems probable that Kettledrummle allotted this part in the success to his companions in adversity, lest they should be tempted to disclose his carnal self-seeking and falling away, in regarding too closely his own personal safety. These strong testimonies in favour of the liberated captives quickly flew abroad with many exaggerations among the victorious army. The reports on the subject were various; but it was universally agreed, that young Morton of Milnwood, the son of the stout soldier of the Covenant, Silas Morton, together with the precious Gabriel Kettledrummle, and a singular devout Christian woman, whom many thought as good as himself at extracting a doctrine or an use, whether of terror or consolation, had arrived to support the good old cause, with a reinforcement of a hundred well-armed men from the Middle Ward.

CHAPTER XVIII.

When pulpit, drum ecclesiastic,
Was beat with fist instead of a stick.   *Hudibras.*

IN the mean time, the insurgent cavalry returned from the pursuit, jaded and worn out with their unwonted efforts, and the infantry assembled on the ground which they had won, fatigued with toil and hunger. Their success, however, was a cordial to every bosom, and seemed even to serve in the stead of food and refreshment. It was, indeed, much more brilliant than they durst have ventured to anticipate: for, with no great loss on their part, they had totally routed a regiment of picked men, commanded by the first officer in Scotland, and one whose very name had long been a terror to them. Their success seemed even to have upon their spirits the effect of a sudden and violent surprise, so much had their taking up arms been a measure of desperation rather than of hope. Their meeting was also casual, and they had hastily arranged themselves under such commanders as were remarkable for zeal and courage, without much respect to any other qualities. It followed, from this state of disorganization, that the whole army appeared at once to resolve itself into a general committee for considering what steps were to be taken in consequence of their success, and no opinion could be started so wild that it had not some favourers and advocates. Some proposed they should march to Glasgow, some to Hamilton, some to Edinburgh, some to London. Some were for sending a deputation of their number to London to convert Charles II to a sense of the error of his ways, and others, less charitable, proposed either to call a new successor to the crown, or to declare Scotland a free republic. A free parliament of the nation, and a free assembly of the kirk, were the objects of the more sensible and moderate of the party. In the meanwhile, a clamour arose among the soldiers for bread and other necessaries, and while all complained of hardship and hunger, none took the necessary measures to procure supplies. In short, the camp of the Covenanters, even in the very moment of success, seemed about to dissolve like a rope of sand, from want of the original principles of combination and union.

Burley, who had now returned from the pursuit, found his followers in this distracted state. With the ready talent of one accustomed to encounter exigencies, he proposed, that one hundred of the freshest men should be drawn out for duty—that a small number of those who had hitherto acted as leaders, should constitute a committee of direction until officers should be regularly chosen—and that, to crown the victory, Gabriel Kettledrummle should be called upon to improve the providential success which they had obtained, by a word in season addressed to the army. He reckoned very much, and not without reason, on this last expedient, as a means of engaging the attention of the bulk of the insurgents, while he himself, and two or three of their leaders, held a private council-of-war, undisturbed by the discordant opinions or senseless clamour of the general body.

Kettledrummle more than answered the expectations of Burley. Two mortal hours did he preach at a breathing; and certainly no lungs, or doctrine, excepting his own, could have kept up, for so long a time, the attention of men in such precarious circumstances. But he possessed in perfection a sort of rude and familiar eloquence peculiar to the preachers of that period, which, though it would have been fastidiously rejected by an audience which possessed any portion of taste, was a cake of the right leaven for the palates of those whom he now addressed. His text was from the forty-ninth chapter of Isaiah.

‘ Even the captives of the mighty shall be taken away, and the prey of the terrible shall be delivered, for I will contend with them that contend with thee, and I will save thy children.

' And I will feed them that oppress thee with their own flesh, and they shall be drunken with their own blood as with sweet wine, and all flesh shall know that I the Lord am thy Saviour, and thy Redeemer, the Mighty One of Jacob.'

The discourse which he pronounced upon this subject was divided into fifteen heads, each of which was garnished with seven uses of application; two of consolation, two of terror, two declaring the causes of backsliding and of wrath, and one announcing the promised and expected deliverance. The first part of his text he applied to his own deliverance and that of his companions, and took occasion to speak a few words in praise of young Milnwood, of whom, as of a champion of the Covenant, he augured great things. The second part he applied to the punishments which were about to fall upon the persecuting government. At times he was familiar and colloquial; now he was loud, energetic, and boisterous;—some parts of his discourse might be called sublime, and others sunk below burlesque. Occasionally he vindicated with great animation the right of every freeman to worship God according to his own conscience; and presently he charged the guilt and misery of the people on the awful negligence of their rulers, who had not only failed to establish presbytery as the national religion, but had tolerated sectaries of various descriptions, Papists, Prelatists, Erastians assuming the name of Presbyterians, Independants, Socinians, and Quakers; all of whom, Kettledrummle proposed, by one sweeping act, to expel from the land, and thus re-edify

in its integrity the beauty of the sanctuary. He
next handled very pithily the doctrine of defensive
arms and of resistance to Charles II, observing,
that instead of a nursing father to the Kirk, that
monarch had been a nursing father to none but his
own bastards. He went at some length through the
life and conversation of that joyous prince, few parts
of which, it must be owned, were qualified to stand
the rough handling of so uncourtly an orator, who
conferred on him the hard names of Jeroboam,
Omri, Ahab Shallum, Pekah, and every other evil
monarch recorded in the Chronicles, and concluded
with a round application of the Scripture, ' Tophet
is ordained of old; yea, for the KING it is provided:
he hath made it deep and large: the pile thereof is
fire and much wood: the breath of the Lord, like a
stream of brimstone, doth kindle it.'

Kettledrummle had no sooner ended his sermon,
and descended from the huge rock which had served him for a pulpit, than his post was occupied by
a pastor of a very different description. The reverend Gabriel was advanced in years, somewhat cor-
pulent, with a loud voice, a square face, and a set
of stupid and unanimated features, in which the body seemed more to predominate over the spirit than
was seemly in a sound divine. The youth who succeeded him in exhorting this extraordinary convo-
cation, was hardly twenty years old, yet his thin
features already indicated, that a constitution, naturally hectic, was worn out by vigils, by fasts, by the
rigour of imprisonment, and the fatigues incident to
a fugitive life. Young as he was, he had been twice
imprisoned for several months, and suffered many
severities, which gave him great influence with

those of his own sect.   He threw his faded eyes over the multitude and over the scene of battle, and a light of triumph arose in his glance; his pale yet striking features were coloured with a transient and hectic blush of joy.   He folded his hands, raised his face to Heaven, and seemed lost in mental prayer and thanksgiving ere he addressed the people.   When he spoke, his faint and broken voice seemed at first inadequate to express his conceptions.   But the deep silence of the assembly, the eagerness with which the ear gathered every word, as the famished Israelites collected the heavenly manna, had a corresponding effect upon the preacher himself.   His words became more distinct, his manner more earnest and energetic; it seemed as if religious zeal was triumphing over bodily weakness and infirmity.   His natural eloquence was not altogether untainted with the coarseness of his sect, and yet, by the influence of a good natural taste, it was freed from the grosser and more ludicrous errors of his contemporaries; and the language of Scripture, which, in their mouths, was sometimes degraded by misapplication, gave, in Mackbriar's exhortation, a rich and solemn effect, like that which is produced by the beams of the sun streaming through the storied representation of saints and martyrs on the Gothic window of some ancient cathedral.

He painted the desolation of the church, during the late period of her distresses, in the most affecting colours.   He described her, like Hagar watching the waning life of her infant amid the fountainless desert; like Judah, under her palm-tree, mourning for the devastation of her temple; like Rachael, weeping for her children and refusing comfort. But he chiefly rose into rough sublimity when addressing the men yet reeking from battle. He called on them to remember the great things which God had done for them, and to persevere in the career which their victory had opened.

'Your garments are dyed—but not with the juice of the wine-press; your swords are filled with blood,' he exclaimed, 'but not with the blood of goats or lambs; the dust of the desert on which ye stand is made fat with gore, but not with the blood of bullocks, for the Lord hath a sacrifice in Bozrah, and a great slaughter in the land of Idumea. These were not the firstlings of the flock, the small cattle of burnt-offerings, whose bodies lie like dung on the ploughed field of the husbandman; this is not the savour of myrrh, of frankincense, or of sweet herbs, that is steaming in your nostrils; but these bloody trunks are the carcases of those that held the bow and the lance, who were cruel and would show no mercy, whose voice roared like the sea, who rode upon horses, every man in array as if to battle—they are the carcases even of the mighty men of war that came against Jacob in the day of his deliverance, and the smoke is that of the devouring fires that have consumed them. And those wild hills that surround you are not a sanctuary planked with cedar and plated with silver; nor are ye ministering priests at the altar, with censors and with torches; but ye hold in your hands the sword and the bow, and the weapons of death—And yet verily, I say unto you, that not when the ancient Temple was in its first glory was there offered sacrifice more acceptable than that which you have this day presented, giving to the slaughter the tyrant and the oppressor, with the rocks for your altars, and the sky for your vaulted sanctuary, and your own good swords for the instruments of sacrifice. Leave not, therefore, the plough in the furrow—turn not back from the path in which you have entered, like the famous worthies of old, whom God raised up for the glorifying of his name and the deliverance of his afflicted people—halt not in the race you are running, lest the latter end should be worse than the beginning. Wherefore, set up a standard in the land; blow a trumpet upon the mountains; let not the shepherd tarry by his sheepfold, or the seedsman continue in the ploughed field, but make the watch strong, sharpen the arrows, burnish the shields, name ye the captains of thousands, and captains of hundreds, of fifties, and of tens; call the footmen like the rushing of winds, and cause the horsemen to come up like the sound of many waters, for the passages of the destroyers are stopped, their rods are burned, and the face of their men of battle hath been turned to flight. Heaven has been with you, and has broken the bow of the mighty; then let every man's heart be as the heart of the valiant Maccabeus, every man's hand as the hand of the mighty Sampson, every man's sword as that of Gideon, which turned not back from the slaughter; for the banner of Reformation is spread abroad on the mountains in its first loveliness, and the gates of hell shall not prevail against it.

' Well is he this day that shall barter his house for a helmet, and sell his garment for a sword, and cast in his lot with the children of the Covenant, even to the fulfilling of the promise; and woe, woe unto

him who, for carnal ends and self-seeking, shall
withhold himself from the great work, for the curse
shall abide with him, even the bitter curse of Meroz,
because he came not to the help of the Lord against
the mighty.   Up then, and be doing; the blood of
martyrs, reeking upon scaffolds, is crying for vengeance; the bones of saints, which lie whitening in
the highways, are pleading for retribution; the groans
of innocent captives from desolate isles of the sea,
and from the dungeons of the tyrants' high places,
cry for deliverance; the prayers of persecuted
Christians, sheltering themselves in dens and deserts from the swords of their persecutors, famished with hunger, starving with cold, lacking fire,
food, shelter, and clothing, because they serve God
rather than man—all are with you, pleading, watching, knocking, storming the gates of heaven in your
behalf. Heaven itself shall fight for you, as the stars
in their courses fought against Sisera. Then whoso
will deserve immortal fame in this world, and eternal happiness in that which is to come, let them enter into God's service, and take arles at the hand of
his servant,—a blessing, namely, upon him and his
household, and his children, to the ninth generation;
even the blessing of the promise, for ever and ever!
Amen.'

The eloquence of the preacher was rewarded by
the deep hum of stern approbation which resounded
through the armed assemblage at the conclusion of
an exhortation so well suited to that which they had
done, and that which remained for them to do. The
wounded forgot their pain, the faint and hungry
their fatigues and privations, as they listened to
doctrines which elevated them alike above the wants

and calamities of the world, and identified their cause with that of the Deity. Many crowded around the preacher, as he descended from the eminence on which he stood, and, clasping him with hands on which the gore was yet hardened, pledged their sacred vow that they would play the part of heaven's true soldiers. Exhausted by his own enthusiasm, and by the animated fervour which he had exerted in his discourse, the preacher could only reply, in broken accents,—God bless you, my brethren—it is HIS cause.—Stand strongly up and play the men— the worst that can befal us is but a brief and bloody passage to heaven.'

Balfour, and the other leaders, had not lost the time which was employed in these spiritual exercises. Watch-fires were lighted, centinels were posted, and arrangements were made to refresh the army with such provisions as had been hastily collected from the nearest farm-houses and villages. The present necessity thus provided for, they turned their thoughts to the future. They had despatched parties to spread the news of their victory, and to obtain, either by force or favour, supplies of what they stood most in need. In this they had succeeded beyond their hopes, having at one village seized a small magazine of provisions, forage, and ammunition, which had been provided for the royal forces. This success not only gave them relief at the time, but such hopes for the future, that whereas formerly some of their number began to slacken in their zeal, they now unanimously resolved to abide together in arms, and commit themselves and their cause to the event of war.

And whatever may be thought of the extravagance or narrow-minded bigotry of many of their tenets, it is impossible to deny the praise of devoted courage to a few hundred peasants, who, without leaders, without money, without magazines, without any fixed plan of action, and almost without arms, borne out only by their innate zeal, and a detestation of the oppression of their rulers, ventured to declare open war against an established government, supported by a regular army, and the whole force of three kingdoms.

CHAPTER XIX.

Why, then, say an old man can do somewhat.
Henry IV. Part II.

We must now return to the Tower of Tillietudlem, which the march of the Life-Guards, on the morning of this eventful day, had left to silence and anxiety. The assurances of Lord Evandale had not succeeded in quelling the apprehensions of Edith. She knew him generous, and faithful to his word; but it seemed too plain that he suspected the object of her intercession to be a successful rival; and was it not expecting from him an effort above human nature, to suppose that he was to watch over Morton's safety, and rescue him from all the dangers to which his state of imprisonment, and the suspicions which he had incurred, must repeatedly expose him? She therefore resigned herself to the most heart-rending apprehensions, without admitting, and in-

deed almost without listening to, the multifarious
grounds of consolation which Jenny Dennison
brought forward, one after another, like a skillful
general, who charges with the several divisions of
his troops in regular succession.

First, Jenny was morally positive that young
Milnwood would come to no harm—then, if he did,
there was consolation in the reflection, that Lord
Evandale was the better and more appropriate match
of the two—then, there was every chance of a battle in which the said Lord Evandale might be killed, and there wad be nae mair fash about that job—
then, if the whigs gat the better, Milnwood and
Cuddie might come to the Castle, and carry off the
beloved of their hearts by the strong hand.

‘ For I forget to tell ye, madam,’ continued the
damsel, putting her handkerchief to her eyes, ‘ that
puir Cuddie’s in the hands of the Philistines as weel
as young Milnwood, and he was brought here a
prisoner this morning, and I was fain to speak Tam
Halliday fair, and fleech him, to let me near the puir
creature; but Cuddie wasna sae thankfu’ as he need-
ed till hae been neither,’ she added, and at the same
time changed her tone, and briskly withdrew the
handkerchief from her face; ‘ so I will ne’er waste
my e’en wi’ greeting about the matter. There wad
be aye enow o’ young men left if they were to hang
the tae half o’ them.’

The other inhabitants of the Castle were also in
a state of dissatisfaction and anxiety. Lady Margaret thought that Colonel Grahame, in commanding an execution at the door of her house, and refusing to grant a reprieve at her request, had fallen

short of the deference due to her rank, and had even encroached on her seignorial rights.

'The Colonel,' she said, 'ought to have remembered, brother, that the barony of Tillietudlem has the baronial privilege of pit and gallows, and therefore, if the lad was to be executed on my estate, (which I consider as an unhandsome thing, seeing it is in the possession of females, to whom such tragedies cannot be acceptable) he ought, at common law, to have been delivered up to my baillie, and justified at his sight.'

'Martial law, sister,' answered Major Bellenden, ' supersedes every other.   But I must own I think Colonel Grahame rather deficient in attention to you; and I am not over and above pre-eminently flattered by his granting to young Evandale (I suppose because he is a lord and has interest with the privy-council) a request which he refused to so old a servant of the king as I am.   But so long as the poor young fellow's life is saved, I can comfort myself with the fag end of a ditty as old as myself.' And therewithal, he hummed a stanza:——

'And what though winter will pinch severe
  Through locks of gray and a cloak that's old,
Yet keep up thy heart, bold cavalier,
  For a cup of sack shall fence the cold.'

'I must be your guest here to-day, sister.   I wish to hear the issue of this gathering on Loudon-hill, though I cannot conceive their standing a body of horse appointed like our guests this morning. —Woes me, the time has been that I would have liked ill to have sate in biggit wa's waiting for the news of a skirmish to be fought within ten miles of me! But, as the old song goes,

'For time will rust the brightest blade,
   And years will break the strongest bow;
Was never wight so starkly made,
   But time and years would overthrow.'

' We are well pleased you will stay, brother,'
said Lady Margaret; ' I will take my old privilege
to look after my household, whom this collation has
thrown into some disorder, although it is uncivil to
leave you alone.'

' O, I hate ceremony as I hate a stumbling horse,'
replied the Major. ' Besides, your person would
be with me, and your mind with the cold meat and
reversionary pasties.—Where is Edith?'

' Gone to her room a little evil-disposed, I am
informed, and laid down in her bed for a gliff,' said
her grandmother; ' as soon as she wakes, she shall
take some drops.'

' Pooh! pooh! she's only sick of the soldiers,' answered Major Bellenden.—' She's not accustomed
to see one acquaintance led out to be shot, and another marching off to actual service with some chance
of not finding his way back again. She would soon
be used to it, if the civil war were to break out
again.'

' God forbid, brother!' said Lady Margaret.

' Ay, Heaven forbid, as you say—and, in the
mean time, I'll take a hit at trick-track with Harrison.'

' He has ridden out, sir,' said Gudyill, ' to try if
he can hear ony tidings of the battle.'

' D——n the battle,' said the Major; ' it puts this
family as much out of order as if there had never
been such a thing in the country before—and yet
there was such a place as Kilsythe, John.'

' Ay, and as Tippermuir, your honour,' replied

Gudyill, ' where I was his honour, my late master's, rear rank man.'

' And Alford, John, where I commanded the horse; and Innerlchy, where I was the great Marquis's aid-de-camp; and Auld Earn, and Brig o' Dee.'

' And Philiphaugh, your honour,' said John.

' Umph!' replied the Major; ' the less, John, we say about that matter the better.'

However, being once fairly embarked on the subject of Montrose's campaign, the Major and John Gudyill carried on the war so stoutly, as for a considerable time to keep at bay the formidable enemy called Time, with whom retired veterans, during the quiet close of a bustling life, usually wage an unceasing hostility.

It has been frequently remarked, that the tidings of important events fly with a celerity almost beyond the power of credibility, and that reports, correct in the general point, though inaccurate in details, precede the certain intelligence, as if carried by the birds of the air. Such rumours anticipate the reality, not unlike to the ' shadows of coming events' which occupy the imagination of the Highland Seer. Harrison, in his ride, encountered some such report concerning the event of the battle, and turned his horse back to Tillietudlem in great dismay. He made it his first business to seek out the Major, and interrupted him in the midst of a prolix account of the siege and storm of Dundee, with the ejaculation, ' Heaven send, Major, that we do not see a siege of Tillietudlem before we are many days older.'

' How is that, Harrison?—what the devil do you mean?' exclaimed the astonished veteran.

' Troth, sir, there is strong and increasing belief that Claver'se is clean broken, some say killed; that the soldiers are all dispersed, and that the rebels are hastening this way, threatening death and devastation to a' that will not take the Covenant.'

' I will never believe that,' said the Major, starting on his feet—' I will never believe that the Life Guards would retreat before rebels;—and yet why need I say that,' he continued, checking himself, ' when I have seen such sights myself?—Send out Pike, and one or two of the servants, for intelligence, and let all the men in the Castle and in the village that can be trusted take up arms. This old tower may hold them play a bit, if it were but victualled and garrisoned, and it commands the pass between the high and low countries.—It's lucky I was here.—Go, muster men, Harrison. You, Gudyill, look what provisions you have or can get brought in, and be ready, if the news be confirmed, to knock down as many bullocks as you have salt for.—The well never goes dry.—There are some old-fashioned guns on the battlements; if we had but ammunition, we should do well enough.'

' The soldiers left some casks of ammunition at the Grange this morning, to bide their return,' said Harrison.

' Hasten, then,' said the Major, ' and bring it into the Castle, with every pike, sword, pistol, or gun, that is within our reach; don't leave so much as a bodkin—lucky that I was here.—I will speak to my sister instantly.'

Lady Margaret Bellenden was astounded at intelligence so unexpected and so alarming. It had seemed to her that the imposing force which had that morning left her walls, was sufficient to have routed all the disaffected in Scotland, if collected in a body; and her first reflection was upon the inadequacy of their own means of resistance, to an army strong enough to have defeated Claverhouse and such select troops.

'Woes me! woes me!' said she; 'what will all that we can do avail us, brother?——What will resistance do but bring sure destruction on the house, and on the bairn Edith; for, God knows, I think nae on my ain auld life.'

'Come, sister,' said the Major, 'you must not be cast down; the place is strong, the rebels ignorant and ill-provided: my brother's house shall not be made a den of thieves and rebels while old Miles Bellenden is in it. My hand is weaker than it was, but I thank my old gray hairs that I have some knowledge of war yet. Here comes Pike with intelligence.——What news, Pike? another Philiphaugh job, eh?'

'Ay, ay,' said Pike, composedly; 'a total scattering.——I thought this morning little gude would come of their new-fangled gate of slinging their carabines.'

'Whom did you see?——Who gave you the news?' asked the Major.

'O, mair than half-a-dozen dragoon fellows that are a' on the spur whilk to get first to Hamilton. They'll win the race, I warrant them, win the battle wha like.'

'Continue your preparations, Harrison; get your ammunition in, and the cattle killed. Send down to the borough-town for what meat you can get in. We must not lose an instant.——Had not Edith and you, sister, better return to Charnwood, while we have the means of sending you there?'

' No, brother,' said Lady Margaret, looking very pale, but speaking with the greatest composure; ' since the auld house is to be held out, I will take my chance in it; I have fled twice from it in my days, and I have aye found it desolate of its bravest and its bonniest when I returned, sae that I will e'en abide now, and end my pilgrimage in it.'

' It may, on the whole, be the safest course both for Edith and you,' said the Major; ' for the whigs will rise all the way between this and Glasgow, and make your travelling there, or your dwelling at Charnwood, very unsafe.'

' So be it then,' said Lady Margaret; ' and, dear brother, as the nearest blood-relation of my deceased husband, I deliver to you, by this symbol,'—(here she gave into his hand the venerable gold-headed staff of the deceased Earl of Torwood)—' the keeping and government and seneschal-ship of my Tower of Tillietudlem, and the appurtenances thereof, with full power to kill, slay, and damage those who shall assail the same, as freely as I might do myself. And I trust you will so defend it, as becomes a house in which his most sacred majesty has not disdained'——

' Pshaw! sister,' interrupted the Major, ' we have no time to speak about the king and his breakfast just now!'

And, hastily leaving the room, he hurried, with all the alertness of a young man of twenty-five, to examine the state of his garrison, and superintend the measures which were necessary for defending the place.

The Tower of Tillietudlem, having very thick walls, and very narrow windows, having also a very strong court-yard wall, with flanking turrets on the only accessible side, and rising on the other from the very verge of a precipice, was fully capable of defence against any thing but a train of heavy artillery.

Famine or escalade was what the garrison had chiefly to fear. For artillery, the top of the Tower was mounted with some antiquated wall-pieces, and small cannons, which bore the old-fashioned names of culverins, sakers, demi-sakers, falcons, and falconets. These, the Major, with the assistance of John Gudyill, caused to be scaled and loaded, and pointed them so as to command the road over the brow of the opposite hill by which the rebels must advance, causing, at the same time, two or three trees to be cut down, which would have impeded the effect of the artillery when it should be necessary to use it. With the trunks of these trees, and other materials, he directed barricades to be constructed upon the winding avenue which rose to the Tower from the high-road, taking care that each should command the other. The large gate of the court-yard he barricadoed yet more strongly, leaving only a wicket open for the convenience of passage. What he had most to apprehend, was the slenderness of his garrison; for all the efforts of the steward were unable to get more than nine men under arms, himself and Gudyill included, so much more popular was the cause of the insurgents than that of the government. Major Bellenden, and his trusty servant Pike, made the garrison eleven in number, of whom one half were old men. The round dozen might indeed have been made up, would lady Margaret have consented that Goose Gibbie should again take up arms. But she recoiled from the proposal, when moved by Gudyill, with such abhorrent recollection of the former achievements of that luckless cavalier, that she declared she would rather the Castle were lost than that he were to be enrolled in the defence of it. With eleven men, however, himself included, Major Bellenden determined to hold out the place to the uttermost.

The arrangements for defence were not made without the degree of fracas incidental to such occasions. Women shrieked, cattle bellowed, dogs howled, men ran to and fro, cursing and swearing without intermission, the lumbering of the old guns backwards and forwards shook the battlements, the court resounded with the hasty gallop of messengers who went and returned upon errands of importance, and the din of warlike preparation was mingled with the sounds of female lamentation.

Such a Babel of discord might have awakened the slumbers of the very dead, and, therefore, was not long ere it dispelled the abstracted reveries of Edith Bellenden. She sent out Jenny to bring her the cause of the tumult which shook the castle to its very basis; but Jenny, once engaged in the bustling tide, found so much to ask and to hear that she forgot the state of anxious uncertainty in which she had left her young mistress. Having no pigeon to dismiss in pursuit of information when her raven-messenger had failed to return with it, Edith was compelled to venture in quest of it out of the ark of her own chamber into the deluge of confusion which overflowed the rest of the castle. Six voices

speaking at once, informed her, in reply to her first
inquiry, that Claver'se and all his men were killed,
and that ten thousand whigs were marching to be-
siege the castle, headed by John Balfour of Burley,
young Milnwood, and Cuddie Headrigg. This
strange association of persons seemed to infer the
falsehood of the whole story, and yet the general
bustle in the castle intimated that danger was certainly apprehended.

'Where is Lady Margaret?' was Edith's second
question.

'In her oratory,' was the reply; a cell adjoining
to the old chapel in which the good old lady was
wont to spend the greater part of the days destined
by the rules of the Episcopal Church to devotional
observances, as also the anniversaries of those on
which she had lost her husband and her children,
and, finally, those hours, in which a deeper and
more solemn address to Heaven was called for, by
national or domestic calamity.

'Where, then,' said Edith, much alarmed, 'is
Major Bellenden?'

'On the battlements of the Tower, madam, pointing the cannon,' was the reply.

To the battlements, therefore, she made her way,
impeded by a thousand obstacles, and found the old
gentleman, in the midst of his natural military ele-
ment, commanding, rebuking, encouraging, instruct-
ing, and exercising all the numerous duties of a
good governor.

'In the name of God, what is the matter, uncle?'
exclaimed Edith.

'The matter, my love?' answered the Major
coolly, as, with spectacles on his nose, he examined

the position of a gun—' the matter?—Why—raise her breech a thought more, John Gudyill—the matter? Why, Claver'se is routed, my dear, and the whigs are coming down upon us in force, that's all the matter.'

' Gracious powers!' said Edith, whose eye at that instant caught a glance of the road which ran up the river, ' and yonder they come.'

' Yonder? where?' said the veteran, and his eyes taking the same direction, he beheld a large body of horsemen coming down the path. ' Stand to your guns, my lads,' was the first exclamation; ' we'll make them pay toll as they pass the heugh.—But stay, stay, these are certainly the Life Guards.'

' O no, uncle, no,' replied Edith; ' see how disorderly they ride, and how ill they keep their ranks; these cannot be the fine soldiers who left us this morning.'

' Ah, my dear girl!' answered the Major, ' you do not know the difference between men before a battle and after a defeat; but the Life Guards it is, for I see the red and blue and the King's colours. I am glad they have brought them off, however.'

His opinion was confirmed as the troopers approached nearer, and finally halted on the road beneath the Tower; while their commanding officer, leaving them to breathe and refresh their horses, hastily rode up the hill.

' It is Claverhouse, sure enough,' said the Major; ' I am glad he has escaped, but he has lost his famous black horse. Let Lady Margaret know, John Gudyill; order some refreshments; get oats for the soldiers' horses; and let us to the hall, Edith, to meet him. I surmise we shall hear but indifferent news.'

⸻

CHAPTER XX.

With careless gesture, mind unmoved,
On rade he north the plain,
His seem in thrang of fiercest strife,
When winner aye the same.   *Hardyknute.*

COLONEL GRAHAME of Claverhouse met the family, assembled in the hall of the Tower, with the same serenity and the same courtesy which had graced his manners in the morning. He had even had the composure to rectify in part the disorders of his dress, to wash the signs of battle from his face and hands, and did not appear more disordered in his exterior than if returned from a morning ride.

' I am grieved, Colonel Grahame,' said the reverend old lady, the tears trickling down her face, 'deeply grieved.'

' And I am grieved, my dear Lady Margaret,' replied Claverhouse, 'that this misfortune may render your remaining at Tillietudlem dangerous for you, especially considering your recent hospitality to the King's troops, and your well-known loyalty. And I came here chiefly to request Miss Bellenden and you to accept my escort (if you will not scorn that of a poor runaway) to Glasgow, from whence I will see you safely sent either to Edinburgh or to Dumbarton Castle, as you shall think best.'

' I am much obliged to you, Colonel Grahame,'
replied Lady Margaret, 'but my brother, Major
Bellenden, has taken on him the responsibility of
holding out this house against the rebels; and, please
God, they shall never drive Margaret Bellenden
from her ain hearth-stane while there's a brave man
that says he can defend it.'

' And will Major Bellenden undertake this?' said
Claverhouse hastily, a joyful light glancing from his
dark eye as he turned it on the veteran,—' Yet why
should I question it? it is of a piece with the rest of
his life.—But have you the means, Major?'

' All, but men and provisions, with which we are
ill supplied,' answered the Major.

' As for men,' said Claverhouse, ' I will leave
you a dozen or twenty fellows who will make good
a breach against the devil. It will be of the utmost
service, if you can defend the place but a week, and
by that time you must surely be relieved.'

' I will make it good for that space, Colonel,' replied the Major, ' with twenty-five good men and
store of ammunition, if we should gnaw the soles of
our shoes for hunger; but I trust we shall get in
provisions from the country.'

' And, Colonel Grahame, if I might presume a
request,' said Lady Margaret, ' I would entreat that
Serjeant Francis Stuart might command the auxilia-
ries whom you are so good as to add to the garrison of our people; it may serve to legitimate his
promotion, and I have a prejudice in favour of his
noble birth.'

' The Serjeant's wars are ended, madam,' said
Grahame, in an unaltered tone, ' and he now needs
no promotion that an earthly master can give.'

VOL. II.   K

'Pardon me,' said Major Bellenden, taking Claverhouse by the arm, and turning him away from the ladies, 'but I am anxious for my friends; I fear you have other and more important loss. I observe another officer carries your nephew's standard.'

'You are right, Major Bellenden,' answered Claverhouse firmly; 'my nephew is no more. He has died in his duty as became him.'

'Great God!' exclaimed the Major, 'how unhappy!—the handsome, gallant, high-spirited youth!'

'He was, indeed, all you say,' answered Claverhouse; 'poor Richard was to me as an eldest son, the apple of my eye, and my destined heir; but he died in his duty, and I—I—Major Bellenden'—(he wrung the Major's hand hard as he spoke)—I live to avenge him.'

'Colonel Grahame,' said the affectionate veteran, his eyes filling with tears, 'I am glad to see you bear this misfortune with such fortitude.'

'I am not a selfish man,' replied Claverhouse, 'though the world will tell you otherwise; I am not selfish either in my hopes or fears, my joys or sorrows. I have not been severe for myself, or grasping for myself, or ambitious for myself. The service of my master and the good of the country is what I have tried to aim at. I may, perhaps, have driven severity into cruelty, but I acted for the best; and now I will not yield to my own feelings a deeper sympathy than I have given to those of others.'

'I am astonished at your fortitude under all the unpleasant circumstances of this affair,' pursued the Major.

'Yes,' replied Claverhouse, 'my enemies in the council will lay this misfortune to my charge—I despise their accusations. They will calumniate me to my sovereign—I can repel their charge. The public enemy will exult in my flight—I shall find a time to show them that they exult too early. This youth that has fallen stood betwixt a grasping kinsman and my inheritance, for you know that my marriage-bed is barren; yet, peace be with him! the country can better spare him than your friend Lord Evandale, who, after behaving very gallantly, has, I fear, also fallen.'

'What a fatal day!' ejaculated the Major. 'I heard a report of this, but it was again contradicted; it was added, that the poor young nobleman's impetuosity had occasioned the loss of this unhappy field.'

'Not so, Major,' said Grahame; 'let the living officers bear the blame, if there be any, and let the laurels flourish untarnished on the grave of the fallen. I do not, however, speak of Lord Evandale's death as certain; but killed, or prisoner, I fear he must be. Yet he was extricated from the tumult the last time we spoke together. We were then on the point of leaving the field with a rear-guard of scarce twenty men; the rest of the regiment were almost dispersed.'

'They have rallied again soon,' said the Major, looking from the window on the dragoons, who were feeding their horses and refreshing themselves beside the brook.

'Yes,' answered Claverhouse, 'my blackguards had little temptation either to desert, or to straggle farther than they were driven by their first panic. There is small friendship and scant courtesy between them and the boors of this country; every

village they pass is likely to rise on them, and so
the scoundrels are driven back to their colours by a
wholesome terror of spits, pike-staves, hay-forks,
and broom-sticks.——But now let us talk about your
plans and wants, and the means of corresponding
with you. To tell you the truth, I doubt being able
to make a long stand at Glasgow, even when I have
joined my Lord Ross; for this transient and acci-
dental success of the fanatics will raise the devil
through all the western counties.'

They then discussed Major Bellenden's means of
defence, and settled a plan of correspondence, in
case a general insurrection took place, as was to be
expected. Claverhouse renewed his offer to escort
the ladies to a place of safety; but, all things considered, Major Bellenden thought they would be in
equal safety at Tillietudlem.

The Colonel then took a polite leave of Lady
Margaret and Miss Bellenden, assuring them, that,
though he was reluctantly obliged to leave them for
the present in dangerous circumstances, yet his earliest means should be turned to the redemption of
his character as a good knight and true, and that
they might speedily rely on hearing from or seeing
him.

Full of doubt and apprehension, Lady Margaret
was little able to reply to a speech so much in unison with her usual expressions and feelings, but
contented herself with bidding Claverhouse farewell, and thanking him for the succours which he
had promised to leave them. Edith longed to inquire the fate of Henry Morton, but could find no
pretext for doing so, and could only hope that it had
made a subject of some part of the long private

communication which her uncle had held with Claverhouse. On this subject, however, she was disappointed; for the old cavalier was so deeply im-
mersed in the duties of his new office, that he had
scarce said a single word to Claverhouse, excepting upon military matters, and most probably would
have been equally forgetful had the fate of his own
son, instead of his friend's, lain in the ballance.

Claverhouse now descended the bank on which
the castle is founded, in order to put his troops
again in motion, and Major Bellenden accompanied
him to receive the detachment who were to be left
in the Tower.

'I shall leave Inglis with you,' said Claverhouse,
'for, as I am situated, I cannot spare an officer of
rank; it is all we can do, by our joint efforts, to keep
the men together. But should any of our missing
officers make their appearance, I authorise you to
detain them, for my fellows can with difficulty be
subjected to any other authority.'

His troops being now drawn up, he picked out
sixteen men by name, and committed them to the
command of Corporal Inglis, whom he promoted
to the rank of serjeant upon the spot.

'And hark ye, gentlemen,' was his concluding
harangue, 'I leave you to defend the house of a
lady, and under the command of her brother, Major Bellenden, a faithful servant of the King. You
are to behave bravely, soberly, regularly, and obe-
diently, and each of you shall be handsomely rewarded on my return to relieve the garrison. In
case of mutiny, cowardice, neglect of duty, or the
slightest excess in the family, the provost-marshal
and cord—you know I keep my word for good and
evil.'

He touched his hat as he bade them adieu, and shook hands cordially with Major Bellenden.

'Adieu,' he said, ' my stout-hearted old friend! Good luck be with you, and better times to us both.'

The horsemen whom he commanded had been once more reduced to tolerable order by the exertions of Major Allan, and, though shorn of their splendour, and with their gilding all besmirched, made a much more regular and military appearance on leaving, for the second time, the Tower of Tillietudlem, than when they returned to it after their rout.

Major Bellenden, now left to his own resources, sent out several videttes, both to obtain supplies of provisions, and especially of meal, and to get knowledge of the motions of the enemy. All the news he could collect on the second subject tended to prove, that the insurgents meant to remain on the field of battle for that night. But they, also, had abroad their detachments and advanced guards to collect supplies, and great was the doubt and distress of those who received contrary orders in the name of the King and in that of the Kirk; the one commanding them to send provisions to victual the castle of Tillietudlem, and the other enjoining them to forward supplies to the camp of the godly-professors of true religion, now in arms for the cause of covenanted reformation, presently pitched at Drumclog, nigh to Loudon-hill. Each summons closed with a denunciation of fire and sword if it was neglected; for neither party could confide so far in the loyalty or zeal of those whom they addressed, as to hope they would part with their property upon other terms. So that the poor people knew not what hand to turn themselves to; and, to say truth, there were some who turned themselves to more than one.

'Thir kittle times will drive the wisest o' us daft,' said Niel Blane, the prudent host of the Howff; 'but I'se aye keep a calm sough.—Jenny, what meal is in the girnel?'

'Four bows o' aitmeal, twa bows o' bear, and twa bows o' pease,' was Jenny's reply.

'Aweel, hinny,' continued Niel Blane, sighing deeply, 'let Bauldie drive the pease and bear meal to the camp at Drumclog—he's a whig, and was the auld gude-wife's pleughman—the mashlum bannocks will suit their moorland stamachs weel. He maun say it's the last unce o' meal in the house, or, if he scruples to tell a lie, (as it's no likely he will when it's for the gude o' the house,) he may wait till Duncan Glen, the auld drucken trooper, drives up the aitmeal to Tillietudlem, wi' my dutifu' service to my Leddy and the Major, and I haena as muckle left as will mak my parritch; and, if Duncan manage right, I'll gi'e him a tass o' whisky shall mak the blue low come out at his mouth.'

'And what are we to eat oursels then, father, when we hae sent awa' the hail meal in the ark and the girnel?'

'We maun gar wheat-flour serve us for a blink,' said Niel, in a tone of resignation; 'it's no that ill food, though far frae being sae hearty or kindly to a Scotchman's stamach as the curney aitmeal is; the Englishers live amaist upon't, but, to be sure, the pock-puddings ken nae better.'

While the prudent and peaceful endeavoured,

like Niel Blane, to make fair weather with both parties, those who had more public (or party) spirit, began to take arms on all sides. The royalists in the country were not numerous, but were respectable from their fortune and influence, being chiefly landed proprietors of ancient descent, who, with their brothers, cousins, and dependants, to the ninth generation, as well as their domestic servants, formed a sort of militia, capable of defending their own peel-houses against detached bodies of the insurgents, of resisting their demand of supplies, and intercepting those which were sent to the presbyterian camp by others. The news that the Tower of Tillietudlem was to be defended against the insurgents, afforded great courage and support to these feudal volunteers, who considered it as a stronghold to which they might retreat, in case it should become impossible for them to maintain the desultory war they were now about to wage.

On the other hand, the towns, the villages, the farm-houses, the properties of small heritors, sent forth numerous recruits to the presbyterian interest. These men had been the principal sufferers during the oppression of the time. Their minds were fretted, soured and driven to desperation, by the various exactions and cruelties to which they had been subjected; and, although by no means united among themselves, either concerning the purpose of this formidable insurrection, or the means by which that purpose was to be obtained, most considered it as a door opened by Providence to obtain the liberty of conscience of which they had been long deprived, and to shake themselves free of a tyranny, directed both against body and soul. Numbers of these men, therefore, took up arms, and, in the phrase of their time and party, prepared to cast in their lot with the victors of Loudon-hill.

CHAPTER XXI.

Ananias. I do not like the man: He's a heathen,
And speaks the language of Canaan truly.
  Tribulation: You must await his calling, and the coming
Of the good spirit. You did ill to upbraid him. *The Alchemist.*

WE return to Henry Morton, whom we left on the field of battle. He was eating, by one of the watch-fires, his portion of the provisions which had been distributed to the army, and musing deeply on the path which he was next to pursue, when Burley suddenly came up to him, accompanied by the young minister, whose exhortation after the victory had produced such a powerful effect.

'Henry Morton,' said Balfour abruptly, 'the council of the army of the covenant, confiding that the son of Silas Morton can never prove a luke-warm Laodicean, or an indifferent Gallio, in this great day, have nominated you to be a captain of their host, with the right of a vote in their council, and all authority fitting for an officer who is to com-mand christian men.'

' Mr. Balfour,' replied Morton, without hesita-tion, ' I feel this mark of confidence, and it is not surprising that a natural sense of the injuries of my country, not to mention those I have sustained in my own person, should make me sufficiently

K 2

willing to draw my sword for liberty and freedom
of conscience.   But I will own to you, that I must
be better satisfied concerning the principles on which
you bottom your cause ere I can agree to take a
command amongst you.'

'And can you doubt of our principles,' answered
Burley, 'since we have stated them to be the reformation both of church and state, the rebuilding of
the decayed sanctuary, the gathering of the dispersed saints, and the destruction of the man of
sin?'

'I will own frankly, Mr. Balfour,' replied Morton, 'much of this sort of language, which I observe, is so powerful with others, is entirely lost on
me.   It is proper you should be aware of this before we commune further together.'   (The young
clergyman here groaned deeply.)   'I distress you,
sir,' said Morton; 'but, perhaps, it is because you
will not hear me out.   I revere the scriptures as
deeply as you or any christian can do.   I look into
them with humble hope of extracting a rule of conduct and a law of salvation.   But I expect to find
this by an examination of their general tenor, and
of the spirit which they uniformly breathe, and not
by wresting particular passages from their context,
or by the application of Scriptural phrases to circumstances and events with which they have often
very slender relation.'

The divine, whose name was Ephraim Macbriar,
seemed shocked and thunder-struck with this declaration, and was about to remonstrate.

'Hush, Ephriam!' said Burley, 'remember he is
but as a babe in swaddling clothes.—Listen to me,
Morton.   I will speak to thee in the worldly

language, of that carnal reason, which is, for the present, thy blind and imperfect guide. What is the object for which thou art content to draw thy sword? Is it not that the church and state should be reformed by the free voice of a free parliament, with such laws as shall hereafter prevent the executive government from spilling the blood, torturing and imprisoning the persons, exhausting the estates, and trampling upon the consciences of men, at their own wicked pleasure?'

'Most certainly,' said Morton; 'such I esteem legitimate causes of warfare, and for such I will fight while I can wield a sword.'

'Nay, but,' said Macbriar, 'ye handle this matter too tenderly, nor will my conscience permit me to fard or daub over the causes of divine wrath'——

'Peace, Ephraim Macbriar,' again interrupted Burley.

'I will not peace,' said the young man. 'Is it not the cause of my master who has sent me? Is not a profane and an Erastian destroying of his authority, usurpation of his power, denial of his name, to place either king or parliament in his place as the master and governor of his household, the adulterous husband of his spouse?'

'You speak well,' said Burley, dragging him aside, 'but not wisely; your own ears have heard this night in council how this scattered remnant are broken and divided, and would ye now make a veil of separation between them? Would ye build a wall with unslacked mortar?—if a fox go up, it will breach it.'

'I know,' said the young clergyman, in reply, 'that thou art faithful, honest, and zealous, even

unto slaying; but, believe me this worldly craft,
this temporizing with sin and with infirmity, is in
itself a falling away, and I fear me Heaven will
not honour us to do much more for his glory, when
we seek to carnal cunning and to a fleshly arm.
The sanctified end must be wrought by sanctified
means.'

'I tell thee,' answered Balfour, 'thy zeal is too
rigid in this matter; we cannot yet do without the
help of the Laodiceans and the Erastians; we must
endure for a space the indulged in the midst of the
council—the sons of Zeruiah are yet too strong for
us.'

'I tell thee I like it not, said Macbriar; 'God can
work deliverance by a few as well as by a multitude. The host of the faithful that was broken
upon Pentland-hills, paid but the fitting penalty of
acknowledging the carnal interest of that tyrant and
oppressor, Charles Stuart.'

'Well, then,' said Balfour, 'thou knowest the
healing resolution that the council have adopted to
make a comprehending declaration, that may suit
the tender consciences of all who groan under the
yoke of our present oppressors. Return to the
council if thou wilt, and get them to recall it, and
send forth one upon narrower grounds. But abide
not here to hinder my gaining over this youth whom
my soul travails for; his name alone will call forth
hundreds to our banners.'

'Do as thou wilt, then,' said Macbriar; 'but I
will not assist to mislead the youth, nor bring him
into jeopardy of life, unless upon such grounds as
will ensure his eternal reward.'

The more artful Balfour then dismissed the impatient preacher, and returned to his proselyte.

That we may be enabled to dispense with detailing at length the arguments by which he urged Morton to join the insurgents, we shall take this opportunity to give a brief sketch of the person by whom they were used, and the motives which he had for interesting himself so deeply in the conversion of young Morton to his cause.

John Balfour of Kinloch, or Burley, for he is designated both ways in the histories and proclamations of that melancholy period, was a gentleman of some fortune, and of good family, in the county of Fife, and had been a soldier from his youth upward. In the younger part of his life he had been wild and licentious, but had early laid aside open profligacy, and embraced the strictest tenets of Calvinism. Unfortunately, habits of excess and intemperance were more easily rooted out of his dark, saturnine, and enterprising spirit, than the vices of revenge and ambition, which continued, notwithstanding his religious professions, to exercise no small sway over his mind. Daring in design, precipitate and violent in execution, and going to the very extremity of the most rigid recusancy, it was his ambition to place himself at the head of the presbyterian interest.

To attain this eminence among the whigs, he had been active in attending their conventicles, and more than once had commanded them when they appeared in arms, and beaten off the forces sent to disperse them. At length, the gratification of his own fierce enthusiasm, joined, as some say, with motives of private revenge, placed him at the head of that

party who assassinated the Primate of Scotland, as
the author of the sufferings of the presbyterians.
The violent measures adopted by government to
revenge this deed, not on the perpetators only, but
on the whole professors of the religion to which
they belonged, together with long previous sufferings, without any prospect of deliverance, except
by force of arms, occasioned the insurrection, which,
as we have already seen, commenced by the defeat
of Claverhouse in the bloody skirmish of Loudon-
hill.

But Burley, notwithstanding the share he had in
the victory, was far from finding himself at the
summit which his ambition aimed at.   This was
partly owing to the various opinions entertained
among the insurgents concerning the murder of
Archbishop Sharpe. The more violent among them
did indeed approve of this act as a deed of justice,
executed upon a persecutor of God's church through
the immediate inspiration of the Deity; but the
greater part of the presbyterians disowned the deed
as a crime highly culpable, although they admitted,
that the Archbishop's punishment had by no means
exceeded his deserts.   The insurgents differed in
another main point, which has been already touched upon. The more warm and extravagant fanatics
condemned, as guilty of a pusillanimous abandon-
ment of the rights of the church, those preachers
and congregations who were contented, in any manner, to exercise their religion through the permission of the ruling government. This, they said, was
absolute Erastianism, or subjection of the church of
God to the regulations of an earthly government,
and therefore but one degree better than prelacy

or popery.—Again, the more moderate party were content to allow the king's title to the throne, and, in secular affairs, to acknowledge his authority, so long as it was exercised with due regard to the liberties of the subject, and in conformity to the laws of the realm. But the tenets of the wilder sect, called, from their leader Richard Cameron, by the name of Cameronians, went the length of disowning the reigning monarch, and every one of his successors who should not acknowledge the Solemn League and Covenant. The seeds of disunison were, therefore, thickly sown in this ill-fated party; and Balfour, however enthusiastic, and however much attached to the most violent of those tenets which we have noticed, saw nothing but ruin to the general cause, if they were insisted on during this crisis, when unity was of so much consequence. Hence he disapproved, as we have seen, of the honest, downright, and ardent zeal of Macbriar, and was extremely desirous to receive the assistance of the moderate party of presbyterians in the immediate overthrow of the government, with the hope of being hereafter able to dictate to them what should be substituted in its place.

He was, on this account, particularly anxious to secure the accession of Henry Morton to the cause of the insurgents. The memory of his father was generally esteemed among the presbyterians; and, as few persons of any decent quality had joined the insurgents, this young man's family and prospects were such as almost ensured his being chosen a leader. Through Morton's means, as being the son of his ancient comrade, Burley conceived he might exercise some influence over the more liberal part of the army, and ultimately, perhaps, ingratiate himself so far with them, as to be chosen commander-in-chief, which was the mark at which his ambition aimed.   He had, therefore, without waiting till any other person took up the subject, exalted to the council the talents and disposition of Morton, and easily obtained his elevation to the painful rank of a leader in this disunited and undisciplined army.

The arguments by which Balfour pressed Morton to accept of this dangerous promotion, as soon as he had gotten rid of his less artful and more uncompromising companion Mackbriar, were sufficiently artful and urgent.   He did not affect either to deny or to disguise that the sentiments which he himself entertained concerning church-government, went as far as those of the preacher who had just left them.   But he argued, that when the affairs of the nation were at such a desperate crisis, minute difference of opinion should not prevent those who, in general, wished well to their oppressed country, from drawing their swords in its behalf.   Many of the subjects of division, as, for example, that concerning the Indulgence itself, arose, he observed, out of circumstances which would cease to exist, provided their attempt to free the country should be successful, seeing that the presbytery, being in that case triumphant, would need to make no such compromise with the government, and, consequently, with the abolition of the Indulgence, all discussion of its legality would be at once ended.   He insisted much and strongly upon the necessity of taking advantage of this favourable crisis, upon the certainty of their being joined by the force of the whole western shires, and upon the gross guilt which those would incur, who, seeing the distress of the country, and the increasing tyranny with which it was governed, should, from fear or indifference, withhold their active aid from the goo cause.

Morton wanted not these arguments to induce him to join in any insurrection, which might appear to have a feasible prospect of freedom to the country. He doubted, indeed, greatly whether the present attempt was likely to be supported by the strength sufficient to ensure success, or by the wisdom and liberality of spirit necessary to make a good use of the advantages that might be gained. Upon the whole, however, considering the wrongs he had personally endured, and those which he had seen daily inflicted on his fellow-subjects; meditating also upon the precarious and dangerous situation in which he already stood with relation to the government, he conceived himself, in every point of view, called upon to join the body of presbyterians already in arms.

But, while he expressed to Burley his acquiescence in the vote which had named him a leader among the insurgents, and a member of their council of war, it was not without a qualification.

'I am willing,' he said, 'to contribute every thing within my limited power to effect the emancipation of my country. But do not mistake me. I disapprove, in the utmost degree, of the action in which this rising seems to have originated, and no arguments should induce me to join it, if it is to be carried on by such measures as that with which it has commenced.'

Burley's blood rushed to his face, giving a ruddy and dark glow to his swarthy brow.

' You mean,' he said, in a voice which he designed should not betray any emotion—' You mean the death of James Sharpe?'

' Frankly,' answered Morton, ' such is my meaning.'

' You imagine, then,' said Burley, ' that the Almighty, in times of difficulty, does not raise up instruments to deliver his church from her oppressors? You are of opinion that the justice of an execution consists, not in the extent of the sufferer's crime, or in his having merited punishment, or in the wholesome and salutary effect which that example is likely to produce upon other evil-doers, but hold that it rests solely in the robe of the judge, the height of the bench, and the voice of the doomster? Is not just punishment justly inflicted, whether on the scaffold or the moor? And where constituted judges, from cowardice, or from having cast in their lot with transgressors, suffer them not only to pass at liberty through the land, but to sit in the high places, and dye their garments in the blood of the saints, is it not well done in any brave spirits who shall draw their private swords in the public cause?'

' I have no wish to judge this individual action,' replied Morton, ' further than is necessary to make you fully aware of my principles. I therefore repeat, that the case you have supposed does not satisfy my judgment. That the Almighty, in his mysterious providence, may bring a bloody man to an end deservedly bloody, does not vindicate those who, without authority of any kind, take upon themselves to be the instruments of execution, nad presume to call them the executors of divine vengeance.'

'And were we not so?' said Burley, in a tone of fierce enthusiasm, 'Were not we—was not every one who owned the interest of the Covenanted Church of Scotland, bound by that covenant to cut off the Judas who had sold the cause of God for fifty thousand merks a-year? Had we met him by the way as he came down from London, and there smitten him with the edge of the sword, we had done but the duty of men faithful to our cause, and to our oaths recorded in heaven. Was not the execution itself a proof of our warrant? Did not the Lord deliver him into our hands, when we looked out but for one of his inferior tools of persecution? Did we not pray to be resolved how we should act, and was it not borne in our hearts as if it had been written on them with the point of a diamond, ' Ye shall surely take him and slay him?'—Was not the tragedy full half an hour in acting ere the sacrifice was completed, and that in an open heath, and within the patroles of their garrisons, and yet who interrupted the great work?—What dog so much as bayed us during the pursuit, the taking, the slaying, and the dispersing? Then, who will say—who dare say, that a mightier arm than ours was not herein revealed?'

'You deceive yourself, Mr. Balfour,' said Morton; 'such circumstances of facility of execution and escape have often attended the commission of the most enormous crimes. But it is not mine to judge you. I have not forgotten that the way was opened to the former liberation of Scotland by an

action of violence which no man can justify;—the
slaughter of Cumming by the hand of Robert
Bruce; and, therefore, condemning this action, as I
do and must, I am not unwilling to suppose that you
may have motives vindicating it in your own eye,
though not to mine, or to those of sober reason.   I
only now mention it, because I desire you to understand, that I join a cause supported by men engaged in open war, which it is proposed to carry on
according to the rules of civilized nations, without,
in any respect, approving of the act of violence
which gave immediate rise to it.'

Balfour bit his lip, and with difficulty suppressed
a violent answer.   He perceived, with disappoint-
ment, that, upon points of principle, his young brother in arms possessed a clearness of judgment, and
a firmness of mind, which afforded but little hope
of his being able to exert that degree of influence
over-him which he had expected to possess.   After
a moment's pause, however, he said, with coolness.
' My conduct is open to men and angels. The deed
was not done in a corner; I am here in arms to
avow it, and care not where, or by whom, I am called on to do so; whether in the council, the field of
battle, the place of execution, or the day of the last
great trial.   I will not now discuss it further with
one who is yet on the outer side of the veil.   But
if you will cast in your lot with us as a brother,
come with me to the council, who are still sitting,
to arrange the future march of the army and the
means of improving our victory.'

Morton arose and followed him in silence, not
greatly delighted with his associate, and better satisfied with the general justice of the cause which

he had espoused, than either with the measures or
motives of many of those who were embarked in it.

CHAPTER XXII.

And look how many Grecian tents do stand
Hollow upon this plain—so many hollow factions.
Troilus and Cressida.

In a hollow of the hill, about a quarter of a mile
from the field of battle, was a shepherd's hut, a miserable cottage, which, as the only enclosed spot
within a moderate distance, the leaders of the presbyterian army had chosen for their council-house.
Towards this spot Burley guided Morton, who was
surprised, as he approached it, at the multifarious
confusion of sounds which issued from its precincts.
The calm and anxious gravity which it might be
supposed would have presided in councils held on
such important subjects, and at a period so critical,
seemed to have given place to discord wild, and
loud uproar, which fell on the ear of their new ally
as an evil augury of their future measures. As they
approached the door, they found it open indeed,
but choked up with the bodies and heads of coun-
try-men, who though no members of the council,
felt no scruple in intruding themselves upon deliberations in which they were so deeply interested. By
expostulation, by threats, and even by some degree
of violence, Burley, the sternness of whose charac-

ter maintained a sort of superiority over these disorderly forces, compelled the intruders to retire,
and, introducing Morton into the cottage, secured
the door behind them against impertinent curiosity.
At a less agitating moment, the young man might
have been entertained with the singular scene of
which he now found himself an auditor and a spectator.

The precincts of the gloomy and ruinous hut
were enlightened partly by some furze which blaz-
ed on the hearth, the smoke whereof, having no legal vent, eddied around, and formed over the heads
of the assembled council a cloudy canopy, as opake
as their metaphysical theology, through which, like
stars through mist, were dimly seen to twinkle a
few blinking candles, or rather rushes dipped in
tallow, the property of the poor owner of the cottage, which were stuck to the walls by patches of
wet clay.   This broken and dusky light showed
many a countenance elated with spiritual pride, or
rendered dark by fierce enthusiasm; and some whose
anxious, wandering, and uncertain looks showed
they felt themselves rashly embarked in a cause
which they had neither courage nor conduct to
bring to a good issue, yet knew not how to abandon,
for very shame. They were, indeed, a doubtful and
disunited body.   The most active of their number
were those concerned with Burley in the death of
the primate, four or five of whom had found their
way to Loudon-hill, together with other men of the
same relentless and uncompromising zeal, who had,
in various ways, given desperate and unpardonable
offence to the government.

With them were mingled their preachers, men who had spurned at the indulgence offered by government, and preferred assembling their flocks in the wilderness, to worshipping in temples built by human hands, if their doing the latter could be construed to admit any right on the part of their rulers to interfere with the supremacy of the Kirk. The other class of counsellors were such gentlemen of small fortune, and substantial farmers, as a sense of intolerable oppression had induced to take arms and join the insurgents. These also had their clergymen with them, who, having many of them taken advantage of the indulgence, were prepared to resist the measures of the more violent, who proposed a declaration in which they should give testimony against the warrants and instructions for indulgence as sinful and unlawful acts. This delicate question had been passed over in silence in the first draught of the manifestos which they intended to publish, of the reasons of their gathering in arms; but it had been stirred anew during Balfour's absence, and, to his great vexation, he now found that both parties had opened upon it in full cry, Macbriar, Kettledrummle, and other teachers of the wanderers, being at the very spring-tide of polemical discussion with Peter Poundtext, the indulged pastor of Milnwood's parish, who, it seems, had e'en girded himself with a broad-sword, but, ere he was called upon to fight for the good cause of presbytery in the field, was manfully defending his own dogmata in the council. It was the din of this conflict, maintained chiefly between Poundtext and Kettledrummle, together with the clamour of their adherents, which had saluted Morton's ears upon approaching the cottage. Indeed, as both the divines were men well gifted with words and lungs, and each fierce, ardent, and intolerant in defence of his own doctrine, prompt in the recollection of texts wherewith they battered each other without mercy, and deeply impressed with the importance of the subject of discussion, the noise of the debate betwixt them fell little short of that which might have attended an actual bodily conflict.

Burley, scandalized at the disunion implied in this virulent strife of tongues, interposed between the disputants, and, by some general remarks on the unseasonableness of discord, a soothing address to the vanity of each party, and the exertion of the authority which his services in that day's victory entitled him to assume, at length succeeded in prevailing upon them to adjourn further discussion of the controversy. But although Kettledrummle and Poundtext were thus for the time silenced, they continued to eye each other like two dogs, who, having been separated by the authority of their masters while fighting, have retreated, each beneath the chair of his owner, still watching each other's motions, and indicating, by occasional growls, by the erected bristles of the back and ears, and by the red glance of the eye, that their discord is unappeased, and that they only wait the first opportunity afforded by any general movement or commotion in the company, to fly once more at each other's throats.

Balfour took advantage of the momentary pause to present to the council Mr. Henry Morton of Milnwood, as one touched with a sense of the evils of the times, and willing to peril goods and life in the precious cause for which his father, the renown-

ed Silas Morton, had given in his time a soul-stir-
ring testimony. Morton was instantly received with
the right hand of fellowship by his ancient pastor,
Poundtext, and by those among the insurgents who
supported the more moderate principles. The others
muttered something about Erastianism, and remind-
ed each other in whispers, that Silas Morton, once
a stout and worthy servant of the Covenant, had
been a backslider in the day when the resolutioners
had led the way in owning the authority of Charles
Stuart, thereby making a gap whereat the present
tyrant was afterward brought in, to the oppression
both of Kirk and country. They added, however,
that, on this great day of calling, they would not refuse society with any who should put hand to the
plough; and so Morton was installed in his office of
leader and counsellor, if not with the full approbation of his colleagues, at least without any formal
or avowed dissent. They proceeded, on Burley's
motion, to divide among themselves the command
of the men who had assembled, and whose numbers
were daily increasing. In this partition, the insurgents of Poundtext's parish and congregation were
naturally placed under the command of Morton; an
arrangement mutually agreeable to both parties, as
he was recommended to their confidence, as well by
his personal qualities as his having been born among
them.

When this task was accomplished, it became necessary to determine what use was to be made of
their victory. Morton's heart throbbed high when
he heard the Tower of Tillietudlem named as one
of the most important positions to be seized upon.
It commanded, as we have often noticed, the pass

between the more wild and the more fertile country, and must furnish, it was plausibly urged, a stronghold and place of rendezvous to the cavaliers and malignants of the district, supposing the insurgents were to march onward and leave it uninvested. This measure was particularly urged as necessary by Poundtext and those of his immediate followers, whose habitations and families might be exposed to great severities, if this strong place were permitted to remain in possession of the royalists.

' I opine,' said Poundtext,—for, like the other divines of the period, he had no hesitation in offering his advice upon military matters of which he was profoundly ignorant,—' I opine, that we should take in and raze that strong-hold of the woman lady Margaret Bellenden, even though we should build a fort and raise a mount against it; for the race is a rebellious and a bloody race, and their hand has been heavy on the children of the Covenant, both in the former and the latter times. Their hook hath been in our noses, and their bridle betwixt our jaws.'

' What are their means and men of defence?' said Burley. ' The place is strong; but I conceive that two women cannot make it good against a host.'

' There is also,' said Poundtext, ' John Gudyill, even the lady's chief butler, who boasteth himself a man of war from his youth upward, and who spread the banner against the good cause with that man of Belial, James Grahame of Montrose.'

' Pshaw!' returned Balfour,' scornfully, ' a butler!'

' Also, there is that ancient malignant,' replied Poundtext, ' Miles Bellenden of Charnwood, whose hands have been dipped in the blood of the saints.'

' If that,' said Burley, ' be Miles Bellenden, the

brother of sir Arthur, he is one whose sword will not turn back from battle; but he must now be stricken in years.'

' There was word in the country as I rode along,' said another of the council, ' that so soon as they heard of the victory which has been given to us, they caused shut the gates of the tower, and called in men, and collected ammunition. They were ever a fierce and a malignant house.'

' We will not, with my consent,' said Burley, ' engage in a siege which may consume time. We must rush forward, and follow our advantage by occupying Glasgow; for I do not fear that the troops we have this day beaten, even with the assistance of my lord Ross's regiment, will judge it safe to await our coming.'

' Howbeit,' said Poundtext, ' we may display a banner before the Tower, and blow a trumpet, and summon them to come forth. It may be that they will give over the place unto our mercy, though they be a rebellious people. And we will summon the women to come forth of their strong-hold, that is, lady Margaret Bellenden and her grand-daughter, and Jenny Dennison, which is a girl of an ensnaring eye, and the other maids, and we will give them a safe conduct, and send them in peace to the city, even to the town of Edinburgh. But John Gudyill, and Hugh Harrison, and Miles Bellenden, we will restrain with fetters of iron, even as they, in times bypast, have done to the martyred saints.'

' Who talks of safe conduct and of peace?' said a shrill, broken, and overstrained voice, from the crowd.

'Peace, brother Habbakuk,' said Macbriar, in a soothing tone to the speaker.

'I will not hold my peace,' reiterated the strange and unnatural voice; 'is this a time to speak of peace, when the earth quakes, and the mountains are rent, and the rivers are changed into blood, and the two-edged sword is drawn from the sheath to drink gore as if it were water, and devour flesh as the fire devours dry stubble?'

While he spoke thus, the orator struggled forward to the inner part of the circle, and presented to Morton's wondering eyes a figure worthy of such a voice and such language. The rags of a dress which had once been black, added to the tattered fragments of a shepherd's plaid, composed a covering scarce fit for the purposes of decency, much less for those of warmth or comfort. A long beard, as white as snow, hung down on his breast, and mingled with bushy, uncombed, grizzled hair, which hung in elf-locks around his wild and staring visage. The features seemed to be extenuated by penury and famine, until they hardly retained the likeness of a human aspect. The eyes, gray, wild, and wandering, evidently betokened a bewildered imagination. He held in his hand a rusty sword, clotted with blood, as were his long lean hands, which were garnished at the extremity with nails like eagles' claws.

'In the name of Heaven! who is he?' said Morton, in a whisper to Poundtext, surprised, shocked, and even startled at this ghastly apparition, which looked more like the resurrection of some cannibal priest, or Druid, red from his human sacrifice, than like an earthly mortal.

' It is Habbakuk Mucklewrath,' answered Pound-text, in the same tone, ' whom the enemy have long detained in captivity in forts and castles, until his understanding hath departed from him, and, as I fear, an evil spirit hath possessed him. Nevertheless, our violent brethren will have it, that he speaketh of the spirit, and that they fructify by his pouring forth.'

Here he was interrupted by Mucklewrath, who cried in a voice that made the very beams of the roof quiver—' Who talks of peace and safe conduct? who speaks of mercy to the bloody house of the malignants? I say, take the infants and dash them against the stones; take the daughters and the mothers of the house and hurl them from the battlements of their trust, that the dogs may fatten on their blood as they did on that of Jezabel, the spouse of Ahab, and that their carcases may be dung to the face of the field even in the portion of their fathers!'

' He speaks right,' said more than one sullen voice from behind; ' we will be honoured with little service in the great cause, if we already make fair weather with Heaven's enemies.'

' This is utter abomination and daring impiety,' said Morton, unable to contain his indignation. ' What blessing can you expect in a cause, in which you listen to the mingled ravings of madness and atrocity?'

' Hush, young man!' said Kettledrummle, ' and reserve thy censure for that for which thou canst render a reason. It is not for thee to judge into what vessels the spirit may be poured.'

'We judge of the tree by the fruit,' said Pound-text, 'and allow not that to be of divine inspiration that contradicts the divine laws.'

'You forget, brother Poundtext,' said Macbriar, 'that these are the latter days, when signs and wonders shall be multiplied.'

Poundtext stood forward to reply; but, ere he could articulate a word, the insane preacher broke in with a scream that drowned all competition.

'Who talks of signs and wonders? Am not I Habbakuk Mucklewrath, whose name is changed to Magr-Missabib, because I am made a terror unto myself and unto all that are around me?—I heard it—When did I hear it?—Was it not in the Tower of the Bass, that overhangeth the wide wild sea?—And it howled in the winds, and it roared in the billows, and it screamed, and it whistled, and it clanged, with the screams and the clang and the whistle of the sea-birds, as they floated, and flew, and dropped, and dived, on the bosom of the waters. I saw it—Where did I see it?—was it not from the high peaks of Dumbarton, when I looked westward upon the fertile land, and northward on the wild Highland hills, when the clouds gathered and the tempest came, and the lightenings of Heaven flashed in sheets as wide as the banners of an host?—What did I see?—Dead corpses and wounded horses, the rushing together of battle, and garments rolled in blood.—What heard I?—The voice that cried, Slay, slay—smite—slay utterly—let not your eye have pity! slay utterly, old and young, the maiden, the child, and the woman whose head is gray—Defile the house and fill the courts with the slain!'

'We receive the command,' exclaimed more than one of the company. 'Six days he hath not spoken nor broken bread, and now his tongue is unloosed! —We receive the command; as he hath said so will we do.'

Astonished, disgusted, and horror-struck, at what he had seen and heard, Morton turned away from the circle and left the cottage. He was followed by Burley, who had his eye on his motions.

'Whither are you going?' said the latter taking him by the arm.

'Any where; I care not whither; but here I will abide no longer.'

'Art thou so soon weary, young man?' answered Burley. Thy hand is but now put to the plough, and wouldst thou already abandon it? Is this thy adherence to the cause of thy father?'

'No cause,' replied Morton, indignantly—'no cause can prosper so conducted—One party declares for the ravings of a blood-thirsty madman; another leader is an old scholastic pedant; a third'—he stopped, and his companion continued the sentence—'is a desperate homicide, thou wouldst say, like John Balfour of Burley?—I can bear thy misconstruction without resentment. Thou dost not consider, that it is not men of sober and self-seeking minds, who arise in these days of wrath to execute judgment and to accomplish deliverance. Hadst thou but seen the armies of England, during her parliament of 1642, whose ranks were filled with sectaries and enthusiasts, wilder than the anabaptists of Munster, thou wouldst have had more cause to marvel; and yet these men were unconquered on the field, and their hands wrought marvellous things for the liberties of the land.'

'But their affairs,' replied Morton, 'were wisely conducted, and the violence of their zeal expended itself in their exhortations and sermons, without bringing divisions into their councils, or cruelty into their conduct. I have often heard my father say so, and protest, that he wondered at nothing so much as the contrast between the extravagance of their religious tenets, and the wisdom and moderation with which they conducted their civil and military affairs. But our councils seem all one wild chaos of confusion.'

'Thou must have patience, Henry Morton,' answered Balfour; 'thou must not leave the cause of thy religion and country either for one wild word, or one extravagant action. Hear me. I have already persuaded the wiser of our friends, that the counsellors are too numerous, and that we cannot expect that the Midianites shall, by so large a number, be delivered into our hands. They have hearkened to my voice, and our assemblies will be shortly reduced within such a number as can consult and act together, and in them thou shalt have a free voice, as well as in ordering our affairs of war, and protecting those to whom mercy should be shown—Art thou now satisfied?'

'It will give me pleasure, doubtless, answered Morton, 'to be the means of softening the horrors of civil war, and I will not leave the post I have taken, until I see measures adopted at which my conscience revolts. But to no bloody executions, after quarter asked, or slaughter without trial, will I lend countenance or sanction; and you may depend on my opposing them, with both heart and hand, as constantly and resolutely if attempted by our own followers, as when they are the work of the enemy.'

Balfour waved his hand impatiently.

' Thou wilt find,' he said, ' that the stubborn and hard-hearted generation with whom we deal, must be chastized with scorpions ere their hearts be humbled, and ere they accept the punishment of their iniquity. The word is gone forth against them, ' I will bring a sword upon you that shall avenge the quarrel of my Covenant.' But what is done shall be done gravely, and with discretion, like that of the worthy James Melvin, who executed judgment on the tyrant and oppressor, Cardinal Beaton.'

' I own to you,' replied Morton, ' that I feel still more abhorrent at cold-blooded and premeditated cruelty, than at that which is practised in the heat of zeal and resentment.'

' Thou art yet but a youth,' replied Balfour, ' and hast not learned how light in the balance are a few drops of blood in comparison to the weight and importance of this great national testimony. But be not afraid; thyself shalt vote and judge in these matters; it may be we shall see little cause to strive together anent them.

With this concession Morton was compelled to be satisfied for the present, and Burley left him, advising him to lie down and get some rest, as the host would probably move in the morning.

' And you,' said Morton, ' do not you go to rest also?'

' No,' said Burley; ' my eyes must not yet know slumber. This is no work to be done lightly; I have yet to perfect the chusing of the committee of lea ders, and I will call you by times in the morning to be present at their consultation.'

He turned away and left Morton to his repose.

The place in which he found himself was not ill adapted for the purpose, being a sheltered nook, beneath a large rock, well protected from the prevailing wind. A quantity of moss with which the ground was overspread, made a couch soft enough for one who had suffered so much hardship and anxiety. Morton wraped himself in the horseman's cloak which he had still retained, stretched himself on the ground, and had not long indulged in melancholy reflections on the state of the country, and upon his own condition, ere he was relieved from them by deep and sound slumber.

The rest of the army slept on the ground, dispersed in groups, which chose their beds on the field as they could best find shelter and convenience. A few of the principal leaders held wakeful conference with Burley on the state of their 'affairs, and some watchmen were appointed who kept themselves on the alert by chanting psalms, or listening to the exercises of the more gifted of their number.

CHAPTER XXIII.

Got with much ease—now merrily to horse.
Henry IV. Part I.

WITH the first peep of day Henry awoke, and found the faithful Cuddie standing beside him with a portmanteau in his hand.

' I hae been just putting your honour's things in readiness again ye were waking,' said Cuddie, ' as is my duty, seeing ye hae been sae gude as to tak me into your service.'

' I take you into my service, Cuddie?' said Morton, ' you must be dreaming.'

' Na, na, sir,' answered Cuddie; ' did-na I say when I was tied on the horse yonder, that if ever ye gat loose I wad be your servant, and ye didna say no? and if that isna hiring, I kenna what is. Ye gae me nae arles, indeed, but ye had gi'en me aneugh before at Milnwood.'

' Well, Cuddie, if you insist on taking the chance of my unprosperous fortunes'——

' Ou ay, I'se warrant us a' prosper well aneugh,' answered Cuddie, cheeringly, ' an' anes my auld mither was weel putten up. I hae begun the campaigning trade at an end that is easy aneugh to learn.'

' Pillaging, I suppose,' said Morton, ' for how else could you come by that portmanteau?'

' I wotna if it's pillaging, or how ye ca't,' said Cuddie, ' but it comes natural to a body, and it's a profitable trade. Our folk had tirled the dead dragoons as bare as bawbees before we were loose amaist—But when I saw the whigs a' weel yokit by the lugs to Kettledrummle and the other chield, I set aff at the lang trot on my ain errand and your honour's. Sae I took up the syke a wee bit, away to the right, where I saw the marks o' mony a horse-foot, and sure aneugh I cam to a place where there had been some clean leatherin', and a' the puir chields were lying there buskit wi' their claes just as they had put them on that morning—naebody had found out that pose o' carcages—and wha suld

be in the midst thereof (as my mither says) but our
auld acquaintance, Serjeant Bothwell?'

' Aye, has that man fallen?' said Morton.

' Troth has he,' answered Cuddie; ' and his e'en
were open, and his brow bent, and his teeth clenged
thegither, like the jaws of a trap for foumarts when
the spring's doun——I was amaist feared to look at
him; however, I thought to hae turn about wi' him,
and sae I e'en riped his pouches, as he had dune
mony an honester man's; and here's your ain siller
again (or your uncle's, which is the same) that he
got at Milnwood that unlucky night that made us a'
sodgers thegither.'

' There can be no harm, Cuddie,' said Morton,
' in making use of this money, since we know how
he came by it; but you must divide with me.'

' Bide a wee, bide a wee,' said Cuddie. ' Weel,
and there's a bit ring he had hinging in a black rib-
bon doun on his breast.　I am thinking it has been
a love-token, puir fallow—there's naebody sae rough
but they hae aye a kind heart to the lasses—and
there's a book wi' a wheen papers, and I gat twa or
three odd things that I'll keep to mysel forby.'

' Upon my word you have made a very successful
foray for a beginner,' said his new master.

' Haena I e'en now?' said Cuddie, with great ex-
ultation. ' I tauld ye I wasna that dooms stupid, if
it cam to lifting things—And forby, I hae gotten
twa gude horse. A feckless loon of a Straven wea-
ver, that had left his loom and his bein house to sit
skirling on a cauld hill-side, had catched twa dragoon naigs, and he could neither gar them hup nor
wind, sae he took a gowd noble for them baith.—
suld hae tried him wi' half the siller, but it's an

unco ill place to get change in—Ye'll find the siller's missing out o' Bothwell's purse.'

'You have made a most excellent and useful purchase, Cuddie; but what is that portmanteau?'

'The pockmantle,' answered Cuddie, 'was lord Evandale's yesterday, and it's yours the day. I fand it ahint the bush o' broom yonder—ilka dog has its day—Ye ken what the auld sang says,

'Take turn about, mother, quo' Tam o' the Linn.'

'And speaking o' that, I maun gang and see about my mother, puir auld body, if your honour hasna ony immediate commands.'

'But, Cuddie,' said Morton, 'I really cannot take these things from you without some recompense.'

'Hout fie, sir,' answered Cuddie, 'ye suld aye be taking,—for recompense, ye may think about that some other time—I hae seen gay weel to mysel wi' some things that fit me better. What could I do wi' lord Evandale's braw claes? Serjeant Bothwell's will serve me weel aneugh.'

Not being able to prevail on his self-constituted and disinterested follower to accept of any thing for himself out of these warlike spoils, Morton resolved to take the first opportunity of returning Lord Evandale's property, supposing him yet to be alive; and, in the meanwhile, did not hesitate to avail himself of Cuddie's prize, so far as to appropriate some change of linen and other trifling articles amongst those of more value which the portmanteau contained.

He then hastily looked over the papers which were found in Bothwell's pocket-book. These were of a miscellaneous description. The roll of his troop, with the names of those absent on furlough, memorandums of tavern-bills, and lists of delinquents who might be made subjects of fine and prosecution, first presented themselves, along with a copy of a warrant from the Privy Council to arrest certain persons of distinction therein named. In another pocket of the book, were one or two commissions which Bothwell had held at different times, and certificates of his services abroad, in which his courage and military talents were highly praised. But the most remarkable paper was an accurate account of his genealogy, with reference to many documents for establishment of its authenticity; subjoined was a list of the ample possessions of the forfeited earls of Bothwell, and a particular account of the proportions in which king James VI had bestowed them on the courtiers and nobility by whose descendants they were at present actually possessed; beneath this list was written, in red letters, in the hand of the deceased, *Haud immemor*, F. S. E. B. the initials probably intimating Francis Stuart, earl of Bothwell. To these documents, which strongly painted the character and feelings of the deceased proprietor of these papers, were added some which showed it in a light greatly different from that in which we have hitherto presented it to the reader.

In a secret pocket of the book, which Morton did not discover without some trouble, were one or two letters, written in a beautiful female hand. They were dated about twenty years back, bore no address, and were subscribed only by initials. Without having time to peruse them accurately, Morton perceived that they contained the elegant yet fond expressions of female affection directed towards an object whose jealousy they endeavoured to sooth, and of whose hasty, suspicious, and impatient temper, the writer seemed gently to complain. The ink of these manuscripts had faded by time, and, notwithstanding the great care which had obviously been taken for their preservation, they were in one or two places chafed so as to be illegible.

' It matters not,' these words were written on the envelope of that which had suffered most, ' I have them by heart.'

With these letters was a lock of hair wrapped in a copy of verses, written obviously with a feeling which atoned, in Morton's opinion, for the roughness of the poetry, and the conceits with which it abounded, according to the taste of the period:—

> Thy hue, dear pledge, is pure and bright,
> As in that well-remember'd night,
> When first thy mystic braid was wove,
> And first my Agnes whisper'd love.
>   Since then how often hast thou press'd
> The torrid zone of this wild breast,
> Whose wrath and hate have sworn to dwell
> With the first sin which peopled hell;
> A breast whose blood's a troubled ocean,
> Each throb the earthquake's wild commotion?—
> O, if such clime thou canst endure,
> Yet keep thy hue unstain'd and pure,
> What conquest o'er each erring thought
> Of that fierce realm had Agnes wrought!
> I had not wander'd wild and wide,
> With such an angel for my guide;

Nor heaven nor earth could then reprove me,
If she had lived, and lived to love me.
   Not then this world's wild joys had been
To me one savage hunting scene,
My sole delight the headlong race,
And frantic hurry of the chace,
To start, pursue, and bring to bay,
Rush in, drag down, and rend my prey,
Then—from the carcase turn away!
Mine ireful mood had sweetness tamed,
And soothed each wound which pride inflamed;
Yes, God and man might now approve me,
If thou hadst lived, and lived to love me!

As he finished reading these lines, Morton could not forbear reflecting with compassion on the fate of this singular and most unhappy being, who, it appeared, while in the lowest state of desperation, and almost of contempt, had his recollections continually fixed on the high station to which his birth seemed to entitle him; and while plunged in gross licentiousness, was in secret looking back with bitter remorse to the period of his youth, during which he had nourished a virtuous, though unfortunate attachment.

'Alas! what are we,' said Morton, 'that our best and most praiseworthy feelings can be thus debased and depraved—that honourable pride can sink into haughty and desperate indifference for general opinion, and the sorrow of blighted affection inhabit the same bosom which licence, revenge, and rapine have chosen for their citadel? But it is the same throughout; the liberal principles of one man sink into cold and unfeeling indifference, the religious zeal of another hurries him into frantic and savage enthusiasm. Our resolutions, our passions,

are like the waves of the sea, and, without the aid
of Him who formed the human breast, we cannot
say to its tides, " Thus far shall ye come, and no
farther.' "

While he thus moralized, he raised his eyes, and
observed that Burley stood before him.

' Already awake?' said that leader—' It is well,
and shows zeal to tread the path before you. What
papers are these?' he continued.

Morton gave him some brief account of Cuddie's
successful marauding party, and handed him the
pocket-book of Bothwell, with its contents. The
Cameronian·leader looked with some attention on
such of the papers as related to military affairs, or
public business; but when he came to the verses, he
threw them from him with contempt.

' I little thought,' he said, ' when, by the blessing
of God, I passed my sword three times through the
body of that arch tool of cruelty and persecution,
that a character so desperate and so dangerous
could have stooped to an art as trifling as it is profane. But I see that Satan can blend the most different qualities in his well-beloved and chosen
agents, and that the same hand which can wield a
club or a slaughter-weapon against the godly in the
valley of destruction, can touch a tinkling lute, or a
gittern, to sooth the ears of the dancing daughters
of perdition in their Vanity Fair.'

' Your ideas of duty, then,' said Morton, ' ex-
clude love of the fine arts, which have been supposed in general to purify and to elevate the mind?'

' To me, young man,' answered Burley, ' and to
those who think as I do, the pleasures of this world,
under whatever name disguised, are vanity, as its

grandeur and power is a snare.   We have but one object on earth, and that is, to build up the temple of the Lord.'

'I have heard my father observe,' replied Morton, 'that many who assumed power in the name of Heaven, were as severe in its exercise, and as unwilling to part with it, as if they had been solely moved by the motives of worldly ambition——But of this another time.   Have you succeeded in obtaining a committee of the council to be nominated?'

'I have,' answered Burley. 'The number is limited to six, of which you are one, and I come to call you to their deliberations.'

Morton accompanied him to a sequestered grass-plot, where their colleagues awaited them. In this delegation of authority, the two principal factions which divided the tumultuary army had each taken care to send three of their own number.   On the part of the Cameronians, were Burley, Macbriar, and Kettledrummle; and on that of the moderate party, Poundtext, Henry Morton, and a small proprietor, called the laird of Langcale.   Thus the two parties were equally balanced by their representatives in the committee of management, although it seemed likely that those of the most violent opinions were as is usual in such cases, to possess and exert the greater degree of energy.   Their debate, however, was conducted more like men of this world than could have been expected from their conduct on the preceding evening.   After maturely considering their means and situation, and the probable increase of their numbers, they agreed that they would keep their position for that day, in order to refresh their men, and give time to reinforcements to join them, and that, on the next morning, they would direct their march towards Tillietudlem, and summon that strong-hold, as they expressed it, of malignancy. If it was not surrendered to their summons, they resolved to try the effect of a brisk assault, and, should that miscarry, it was settled that they should leave a part of their number to blockade the place, and reduce it, if possible, by famine, while their main body should march forward to drive Claverhouse and lord Ross from the town of Glasgow. Such was the determination of the council of management; and thus Morton's first enterprize in active life was likely to be the attack of a castle belonging to the parent of his mistress, and defended by her relative, major Bellenden, to whom he personally owed many obligations. He felt fully the embarrassment of his situation, yet consoled himself with the reflection, that his newly-acquired power in the insurgent army would give him, at all events, the means of extending to the inmates of Tillietudlem a protection which no other circumstance could have afforded them, and he was not without hope that he might be able to mediate such an accommodation betwixt them and the presbyterian army as should secure them a safe neutrality during the war which was about to ensue.

END OF VOL. II.